WONDERS
of the **WINTER**
LANDSCAPE

WONDERS
of the **WINTER**
LANDSCAPE

Shrubs and Trees to Brighten the Cold-Weather Garden

VINCENT A. SIMEONE

{ *Photography by Bruce Curtis, Foreword by Boyce Tankersley, Preface by David Barnett* }

 Ball Publishing | Batavia, Illinois

Ball Publishing
P.O. Box 9
335 N. River Street
Batavia, IL 60510
www.ballpublishing.com

Library of Congress Cataloging-in-Publication Data

Simeone, Vincent A.
  Wonders of the winter landscape : shrubs and trees to brighten the cold-weather garden / Vincent A. Simeone ; photography by Bruce Curtis ; preface by David Barnett ; foreword by Boyce Tankersley.
     p. cm.
  Includes bibliographical references and index.
  ISBN 1-883052-45-9 (hardcover : alk. paper)
  1. Ornamental shrubs. 2. Ornamental trees. 3. Plants in winter. 4. Landscape gardening. I. Title.

SB435.S4839 2005
635.9'76--dc22

                    2005013106

Printed in China by Imago.
9 8 7 6 5 4 3 2 1   05 06 07 08 09 10 11

9749

Dedication

I dedicate this book to my mom, Rosemary Simeone, who encouraged me at a very early age to study horticulture, and to both of my parents, Rosemary and Vincent, who taught me how to enjoy the simple things in life.

Table of Contents

Foreword

In the northern latitudes, winter is the season of long shadows and soft light, cold crisp mornings and early evenings. This is the season for quiet contemplation and appreciation of the landscape at rest. Gone but for the memories are the frantic activities of spring, summer, and early fall.

Shortened days and colder temperatures have stripped the garden down to clean structural lines. The fallen deciduous leaves reveal the beauty of trunk, branch, and bud contrasting with earth, stone, snow, and evergreens. Bird-attractive fruits bedeck trees and shrubs and gleam like jewels in the soft sunlight.

Conifer species with their different foliage colors and textures and distinctively shaped cones move forward to center stage. Summer-green needles turn to bronze, gold, or blue with the onset of cold weather. Cones at maturity take on more obvious colors and open wide to distribute their progeny upon the winter winds.

Broad-leaved evergreens with fat flower buds provide a textural counterpoint to bare branches and coniferous needles. With the onset of colder weather, some seem to draw into themselves while others provide glimpses of unanticipated pigments of earthen tones. On breezy winter days with a bit of sunlight, the waxy coverings of the leaves provide mirrorlike reflections as if to draw the observer closer.

When days warm slightly, witch hazels generously perfume the air with spicy scents and hundreds of luminescent thin-petaled flowers.

These are the pleasures we often miss, and should not.

Boyce Tankersley
Manager of Living Plant Documentation
Chicago Botanic Garden

Preface

Wonders of the Winter Landscape is an excellent resource full of ideas for enhancing the beauty and interest of the winter garden and is bound to inspire many a gardener to more fully appreciate and enjoy the landscape during the cold winter months that make up so much of the year in northern climates. It is unfortunate that most people tend to forget the garden once the temperatures plummet and the snow starts to fall. They are missing so much!

Some of my most memorable moments in "the garden" have occurred just after a fresh snowfall as I walked among the magnificent trees in Mount Auburn Cemetery enjoying the quiet solitude of a cold winter morning. I have also spent many an hour on cold winter days gazing out the window into my backyard garden watching the bird feeder and marveling at the colors and forms of the shrubs as the birds fly back and forth.

Having grown up in New England, I have long appreciated the fact that winter is a wonderful time to observe branching patterns and plant structure, colorful or interesting bark and fruit, and the contrast between evergreen and deciduous trees and shrubs. It is a wonderful time, that is, as long as the landscape consists of the right combination of plants. In this book, Mr. Simeone provides all the information necessary (through photographs, plant names, and accurate descriptions) to create landscapes with true winter interest and appeal.

It takes a certain passion for plants to write a book extolling the virtues of trees and shrubs in the winter, a time when the average person's interest in the garden goes dormant. I have never met anyone with more of this passion than Vincent Simeone.

I can remember the day I first met Vinnie like it was yesterday. The year was 1991, the month was March, and the weather was cold and snowy. He was applying for his first horticultural job, and I couldn't help but notice Vinnie's overflowing enthusiasm for plants. At the time I was the Assistant Director of Planting Fields Arboretum in Oyster Bay, New York. As we talked about the duties and expectations of this job, the "interview" eventually moved outside into the snow for a memorable tour of the plant collections he would soon come to curate, as the decision to hire him came rather quickly and easily.

I have since moved on to Mount Auburn Cemetery back in New England, and Vinnie has climbed the ladder of success at Planting Fields. All these years later his enthusiasm and his knowledge have only grown, and he has done a marvelous job of using those qualities to produce this informative and inspiring book. Read on!

David Barnett
Vice President of Operations & Horticulture
Mount Auburn Cemetery

Acknowledgments

Special thanks to all of the beautiful gardens that inspired the photographs used in this book; Bayard Cutting Arboretum, Bailey Arboretum, Hofstra Arboretum, New York Botanical Garden, Portledge School, and Planting Fields Arboretum State Historic Park.

Also, I would like to extend my sincere gratitude to the collaborators on this book; David Barnett, Bruce Curtis, Mary Jean Hunt, Linda Jacks, Joanne Macrelli, Gloria Simeone, and Boyce Tankersley.

Introduction

Creating a garden that is interesting in the winter takes great enthusiasm, patience, and vision. Nature has undoubtedly mastered the art of winter gardening, and even the most expert gardener can learn from the unrestrained beauty around them. The winter season is a magical time that inspires us to appreciate nature and all of its subtle rewards. Unlike other seasons of the year, winter is not a time to anticipate continuous waves of bright, bold colors in the landscape. Rather, it presents an opportunity for the curious gardener to discover the finer details of the landscape. It takes a truly passionate gardener to marvel at the slightest flicker of interest emanating from a few delicate, curled up blossoms or a cluster of shiny red fruit during the coldest part of the year.

A garden that creates excitement during the winter has great depth and character. Unlike any other season of the year, winter defines the essence of a garden. It strips away the layers to reveal the garden's inner soul. Truthfully, there is nothing more enchanting than a garden in winter. A winter garden that is alive with horticultural riches is truly a gift from nature. Winter gardening is a journey that will lift the sprit, feed the soul, and enable us to better appreciate the entire gardening year as a whole. A great garden in winter will undoubtedly show its magnificence other seasons of the year as well. We should embrace this wonderful season and enjoy all of its bountiful rewards. As the novelist Albert Camus said, "In the depths of winter I finally learned that within me there lay an invincible summer."

Wonders of the Winter Landscape is a unique volume, celebrating the virtues of the winter season and all of the horticultural beauty that is associated with it. Its goal is to demystify this underappreciated season and to create excitement for gardening at an unlikely time of the year. Throughout the book, you will find poetic garden quotes to reinforce the effect that winter has on the human spirit. The

> "What fire could ever
> equal the sunshine
> of a winter's day?"
> —*Henry David Thoreau*

information presented in this book is meant to inspire gardeners to utilize the abundant trees and shrubs that are appropriate for the home garden. Readers will marvel at the glorious woody plants that can be used to enhance and extend the gardening season and add function to the landscape. At the same time, it is my sincere hope that gardeners will also grow to appreciate the large, specimen trees that grace our expansive natural and cultivated landscapes. Although these gifts from nature are too large for most residential landscapes, they should be acknowledged for their majesty and noble presence. Whether gazing at a magnificent display of witch hazel blooms or marveling at the grace of a might oak tree, the landscape in winter will undoubtedly offer gardening bliss.

Defining Winter

Winter is truly one of the most beautiful times of the year to appreciate the garden. Although the garden may appear to be resting, it can burst to life with splendor from choice plants highlighted by exquisite winter sunlight. Interesting plant characteristics such as the growth habit, ornamental fruit, and bark become most evident in winter. Conifers and broadleaf evergreens seem to take command of the landscape with their attractive foliage and striking texture. Collectively, trees and shrubs with winter interest will transform the garden into a winter wonderland.

Winter is defined as the season of the year in which the sun shines most obliquely upon any region and is the coldest time of the year. It is often thought of as a time of dormancy, a chance for all living things to rest until the warmth of spring arrives. To gardeners, the arrival of winter typically means that we put the garden to bed and retreat to our homes, where we can take refuge from the cold. We take this time to reflect on the triumphs of the previous summer and autumn seasons and anticipate the glorious opportunities that the following spring will present. But winter also holds many wondrous horticultural treasures that we often take for granted. It can bring hope to gardeners who will revel in the rejuvenation and horticultural rebirth that winter provides. The landscape in winter takes on a whole new personality, especially during the holiday

"Winter is the time for comfort—it is the time for home."
—*Edith Sitwell*

season when many of the plants growing in the garden are used for displays and decorations.

There are several reasons why winter has a unique personality unlike any other season. First, deciduous trees and shrubs shed their leaves in autumn, exposing their form, structure, and stem texture. Bare trees and shrubs in winter represent the "bones," or the foundation, of our landscapes. While dormant, the bare twigs, stems, and leaf buds of woody plants become prominent in the landscape. It is at this time when the true essence of trees and shrubs can be fully appreciated. With the absence of foliage, trees and shrubs can offer a unique presence in the landscape. The bark texture and overall growth habit of the plants emerge as the focal points to the gardener with a keen eye. In addition, some plants exhibit interesting fruit and flowering characteristics that persevere through the winter months when they are least expected. Together, these aesthetic attributes create the highlights of an otherwise naked garden. Careful plant selection is needed in any garden to ensure that collectively plants offer multiple seasons of interest. In addition, evergreens such as hollies, rhododendrons, and spruces seem to come alive with bold foliage texture and vivid colors.

Second, the winter environment enhances the beauty of trees and shrubs in winter. A fresh blanket of snow or a thin layer of ice clinging to the bare branches of a tree will make plants glisten in the winter sun. In addition to the canvas of snow and ice, the natural, soft glowing light of winter can also accentuate the beauty of trees and shrubs. But even a cloudy, winter's day can provide a hauntingly beautiful and mysterious

feeling to the garden. Why the difference in lighting? During the winter months in the Northern Hemisphere, there is less direct sunlight because of the earth's orientation to the sun. The Winter Solstice, December 21 or 22 each year, is the shortest day of the year, when the sun is at its furthest point from the equator. During this time the winter sun can provide a soft hue or a moderate light that is unlike other times of the year. In winter, at any given time of the day plants will fade into the landscape or jump out to the forefront depending on how the light is illuminating them. All of these environmental factors play an important role in the winter landscape.

Appreciating the Total Package

There are a wide variety of ornamental characteristics of woody plants that are highlighted in winter. Among these fine attributes are the unusual and often striking flowers that emerge in winter, though it is hard to imagine flowers unfurling during the cold days of winter.

It is no secret that flowers are the single most popular aesthetic attribute of plants in the garden. During the spring and summer, gardeners pride themselves on the creation of rich color combinations of bright, showy flowers. Although flowers are the most popular attribute of plants, flowers alone do not create a great garden. Because flowers on trees and shrubs normally last only a few weeks, a well-planned garden should also emphasize other aesthetic attributes of plants such as foliage, fruit, bark, and overall growth pattern.

While flowers are an important feature of woody plants, they are only one of many facets of a plant's ornamental value. There are many worthy tree and shrub species that can be used in the garden that have much to offer in addition to flowers. For example, Japanese stewartia (*Stewartia pseudocamellia*) is a four-season plant offering beautiful white flowers with bright yellow centers in early summer. However, stewartia's best attributes are in the fall and winter, when leaves turn crimson red and the smooth mottled bark with tones of gray, brown, and beige are most noticeable. Anytime of the year that you gaze at a stewartia, you will enjoy unparalleled beauty.

Throughout this book, numerous important aesthetic attributes of a wide variety of choice woody plants are presented. Whether it's a spectacular display of flowers or fruit of an outstanding shrub or the beautifully crafted growth habit of a deciduous tree with interesting architectural form, plants dazzle us with their unbridled beauty.

Simply put, winter is nature's poetry, sprinkling its magic throughout the landscape like an artist's paintbrush swirling across a canvas. The winter garden can stir many emotions within us all, but none is more potent than the comfort it brings knowing the garden is alive with horticultural riches. Winter soothes our souls and allows us as gardeners to reach for new beginnings and anticipate all that the garden can be. Gardening is an endless and wonderful journey that makes the world around us a better place.

Using Plant Names

Both scientific plant names and common names are important parts of everyday gardening life. Scientific

> "The gardening season officially begins on January 1st and ends on December 31."
> —*Marie Huston*

names are written in Latin, which is considered a universal language in the horticultural world. These scientific names are comprised of a genus, also referred to as generic term, and a specific epithet. A genus is defined as a group of closely related plants comprising one or more species. The second name, a specific epithet, identifies the specific member of a genus. Collectively, the two names represent a particular species. For example, the scientific name for Japanese yew is *Taxus* (genus) *cuspidata* (specific epithet). These plant names are important to understand, especially when researching or purchasing plants from a local nursery or garden center.

In addition to scientific names, plants are also typically assigned common names as well. These names can vary among regions, and individual plants, and plants may even have several common names. For example, *Betula papyrifera* can be referred to as paper birch, canoe birch, or white birch. Common names also typically describe a physical or unique characteristic of a given plant. For example, leatherleaf viburnum (*Viburnum rhytidophyllum*) has rough, leathery leaves

that provide an unmistakable, bold texture in the landscape. Common names tend to create confusion and scientific names are more reliable when identifying plants. It is important for even the casual gardener to learn both scientific and common names.

Public gardens provide an important service as educational facilities to promote the vital role plants play in the environment we live in. Public gardens often label their trees and shrubs with both common and scientific names prominently displayed. In fact, one of the most important elements of a public garden with a strong educational mission is its ability to display readable, coherent plant labels. These horticultural institutions give interested gardeners the opportunity to learn about a variety of complex plants that are suitable for the home landscape.

Other important terms that are helpful to know are cultivars and naturally occurring varieties. A cultivar, also referred to as a cultivated variety or garden variety, is cultivated or selected for certain special garden qualities that are distinctive from the species. Cultivated varieties typically originate in a garden and have very specific ornamental characteristics and landscape function that are valuable in the cultivated garden. Cultivar names are capitalized and are usually surrounded by single quotation marks. Instead of single quotations, you may also find single quotes replaced by the letters cv., which represents the term *cultivated variety*. For example, the scientific name for blue atlas cedar can be written as *Cedrus atlantica* 'Glauca' or *Cedrus atlantica* cv. Glauca. Although the term *variety* in this book commonly refers to garden varieties, the true scientific meaning of the term *variety* represents a naturally occurring variation within a species and is written in lower case letters and without single quotations. For example, *Acer palmatum* var. *dissectum* is the scientific name for cutleaf Japanese maple. It is a true, naturally occurring variety with a lower-growing mounded growth habit and finely cut leaves that is quite different than the straight species (*Acer palmatum*).

Hardiness Zone Map

The USDA Plant Hardiness Zone Map is designed to illustrate the average minimum temperatures of the United States. The map is separated into eleven zones, 1 representing the coldest zone and 11 representing the warmest zone. Although there are other environmental factors that impact plant adaptability—such as heat, humidity, and rainfall—cold hardiness is one of the most important factors influencing plant survival. To use the map, identify the area on the map where you live. There will be a zone number assigned to that region. For example, the hardiness zone for Chicago is Zone 5. For exact temperature ranges within a given hardiness zone, read the zone key located below the map. It is important to identify the zone where you live to ensure that the plants you select will survive in that climate. Selecting plants that are tender or marginally hardy in any given hardiness zone may result in poor performance or death of the plant. The plant hardiness zone range for each plant species or variety is listed within the text of each plant description.

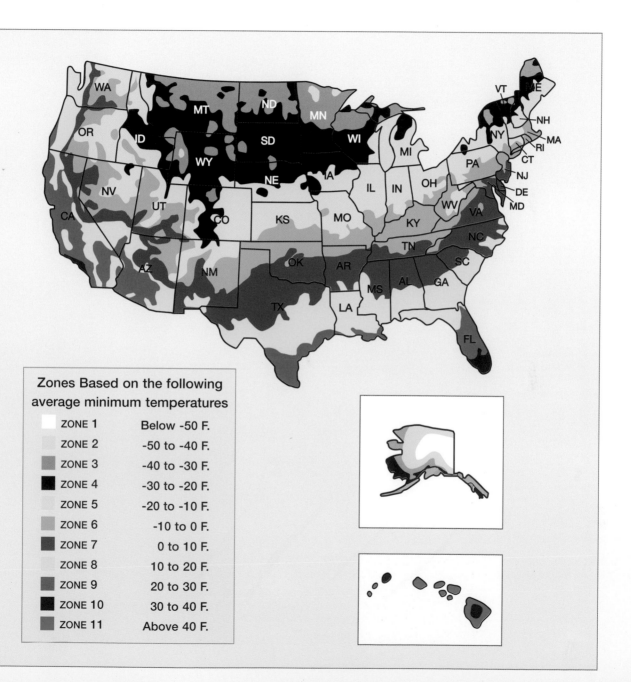

Zones Based on the following
average minimum temperatures

ZONE 1	Below -50 F.
ZONE 2	-50 to -40 F.
ZONE 3	-40 to -30 F.
ZONE 4	-30 to -20 F.
ZONE 5	-20 to -10 F.
ZONE 6	-10 to 0 F.
ZONE 7	0 to 10 F.
ZONE 8	10 to 20 F.
ZONE 9	20 to 30 F.
ZONE 10	30 to 40 F.
ZONE 11	Above 40 F.

Deciduous
Trees and Shrubs

PART 1

This section of the book is devoted to trees and shrubs that shed their leaves in the autumn, exposing their beautiful structure, bare stems, persistent fruit, and even flowers that will develop on certain species. Deciduous plants are defined as plants that shed their leaves annually at the end of growing season in the autumn and will regain them the following spring. Woody plants provide the foundation upon which our great landscapes, manmade or natural, are built. These trees and shrubs offer us something to admire even when there are no leaves to be found in the naked landscape.

Bark, Bark, and More Bark!

CHAPTER 1

Bark texture is undoubtedly one of the most under-appreciated elements of the winter landscape. Yet bark is also one of the most effective and attractive characteristics of plants during the winter. Depending on the species, bark is either a thin or thick protective layer of dead woody tissue that protects the living tissue underneath, which conducts water and nutrients throughout the plant. While bark plays a significant role in protecting the vital living parts of the plant, we also admire it for the beautiful textures and colors that it displays. Whether rough or smooth, the texture of the bark can be especially interesting in the winter. In addition to bark texture, many trees and shrubs also exhibit showy, colorful bark. These colors can range from deep or bright red to golden yellow to silvery gray, depending on the species in question. Often varying bark textures can be found on the same tree, and this differentiation can be quite stunning. For example, the multicolored, exfoliating bark of Japanese stewartia (*Stewartia pseudocamellia*) can have a shaggy outer bark that flakes to reveal a smoother underbark. In many cases, as plants get older their bark interest becomes more prominent. Following is a list of excellent trees and shrubs that are well known for their interesting bark.

"Losing face
is as important to people
as losing bark is to a tree."
—*Chinese proverb*

{ *Acer* spp.
Maples

There are over two hundred species of maples from all over the world, many of which thrive in the United States. There are several species and varieties among this long list of maples that are handsome additions to the winter landscape. Although maples are best known for their lush green leaves and exquisite fall foliage colors, they can also offer an attractive growth habit and textured bark. Depending on the species and variety, maples can offer an assortment of growth patterns from small, dense, rounded canopies to upright, expanding, irregularly spreading branches. The bark can range from smooth and gray in color to deeply fissured, brown bark. In addition, maples develop winged fruit known as samaras that often persist into the winter months. All of these attributes make maples standouts in the winter landscape.

Acer palmatum (Japanese maple)

Maples come in all shapes, sizes, and colors, but no species is more popular than Japanese maple (*Acer palmatum*). Japanese maple is undoubtedly one of the most common maples found in cultivated American landscapes. This Asian species—found growing naturally in the wilds of Japan, central China, and Korea—is one of the most adaptable and diverse of all the maples. Because of its vast aesthetic qualities and versatility, Japanese maple is most appropriate for the home garden. Although a newly planted tree will need some initial care, Japanese maple is quite durable once established. It is well known for its deli-

Coral bark maple's bright red stems

> "The scarlet of the maples
> can shake me like a cry,
> Of bugles going by."
> —*William Bliss Carman*

cate, green, palm-shaped leaves and red fall color. Some varieties will also offer deep, burgundy red leaves during the growing season. But this finely textured plant also exhibits a beautiful smooth, gray bark and a picturesque growth habit that only improves with age. Older specimens develop an oval-to-rounded shape consisting of an array of irregularly growing branches.

One of the most unusual varieties of Japanese maple is the coral bark maple (*Acer palmatum* 'Sango

Kaku'). In the autumn, the delicate leaves of this select variety turn a soft yellow before they fall, exposing the bright, coral red stems. This striking bark color provides a spectacular, glowing effect, especially against a well-contrasted background such as snow or an evergreen tree. This variety is ideal in small groupings or as a single specimen, and will provide a fiery accent to a plain winter landscape. This medium-sized tree will eventually reach 20–25 ft. in height and should be given ample room to grow. It is also effective in a front yard near the foundation of a house, or in the lawn area. For best stem and foliage coloring, this variety should be sited in full sun or partial shade. This winter beauty is truly a stunning addition to the garden. Hardy from Zones 5–8.

In addition to the larger Japanese maple varieties, there are also many varieties of the cutleaf Japanese maple (*Acer palmatum* var. *dissectum*), which has a distinct mounded, sprawling growth habit. The branches, covered with a smooth gray bark, are often twisted and gnarled, displaying a very picturesque and artistic appearance during the winter months. Since this variety does not grow nearly as large as the species, it is very valuable in landscapes with limited space. While this variety also needs ample room, it will typically only reach 10–12 ft. high with a similar spread. All too often this magnificent specimen tree is sited in an inappropriate location with limited room. Regular pruning to keep this tree in scale with its surroundings is really not the best solution, so make sure your maple is sited in an area at least 10 ft.

The beautiful, twisted growth habit of cutleaf Japanese maple creates an impressive display.

Cutleaf Japanese maple's smooth, silvery gray bark

wide. Cutleaf Japanese maple is ideal along the foundation of a house, in a lawn area, or as an accent to a small pond or stream in a woodland garden.

Acer buergerianum (trident maple)

The trident maple is a lesser-known maple species that is gaining in popularity in American gardens. The unusual three-lobed, glossy rich green leaves turn yellow, orange, or red—and sometimes purple—in fall. As the leaves fall, they unveil a gray or light, orange-brown, shaggy bark that becomes rough and plated on established specimens. This beautifully textured bark will flake off in sheets and is quite conspicuous in winter.

Trident maple is an extremely adaptable tree but thrives in full sun or partial shade and well-drained soil. It is very often used in high traffic areas and is tolerant of poor, infertile compacted soil. Trident maple is also very tolerant of drought, heat, and cold climates. In commercial settings it is found in parks or lining a street but is equally effective as a small specimen tree in a residential setting. Trident maple is a delightful medium-sized tree that can grow up to 35 ft. high with half the spread. Trident maple is ideal as a lawn tree, shade tree, or even near a patio where it will cast filtered light. Trident maple is one of the best small trees for the home landscape. Hardy from Zones 5–8 and possibly 9 with careful siting.

Acer griseum (paperbark maple)

Like the name suggests, this plant features a striking, reddish brown peeling bark that is a welcome addition to any winter garden. The dark green leaves are trifoli-ate, which means they are made up of three leaflets, and provide a delicate texture during the summer months. In autumn, the leaves turn crimson red to maroon and eventually drop to reveal the beautiful, papery bark. This elegant specimen tree can reach

The peeling bark of paperbark maple will have garden visitors doing a double take.

20–30 ft. high with a similar spread, but is usually taller than it is wide. The unique thing about this tree is that even the youngest of stems will offer an interesting peeling bark effect.

Although paperbark maple is a slow-growing tree

The beautiful flaking winter trunk of paperbark maple.

that takes a few years to establish, it will only improve with age and provide gardeners with many years of joy as it graces the landscape. While it is most noticeable in winter, paperbark maple is aesthetically pleasing all year round. It is quite adaptable but performs best in full sun or partial shade and well-drained, acidic soils. Hardy from Zones 5–8.

Paperbark maple is an excellent small specimen tree for the front yard or lawn area. It is also effective in a woodland garden in partial shade. This outstanding four-season tree is a must have for gardeners who truly appreciate winter bark interest.

Striped, or snakebark maples

Striped maples are small- to medium-sized trees with green stems and trunks highlighted by prominent white or silver streaks. These noticeable white streaks contrast well against the smooth green bark, and the combination is quite interesting. This bark effect is very pronounced during the winter season. In addition, their dark green leaves emerge in the spring and turn brilliant shades of yellow in the autumn. While there are several species, the most common in cultivation is a species native to the eastern United States, common striped maple, also called moosewood (*Acer pensylvanicum*). There are also several European and Asian species that are gaining in popularity.

The snakebark maples are most suitable as understory trees beneath the shelter and shade of the taller forest canopy. Although they will tolerate full sun, these delightful small to medium sized trees do particularly well in a partially shaded area of the garden with dappled light. For best growth, soil should be moist, well drained, organic, and acidic.

Striped maples are ideal for a shade garden in a woodland type environment. They can be featured as a single specimen or used in small groupings. They should be sited some place close to a path or sitting area where their smooth, colorful bark can be enjoyed close-up. 'White Tigress' is a hybrid striped maple and common garden variety with very pronounced white stripes along the stems and twigs. In general, striped maples are hardy from Zones 3–7.

Acer saccharum (sugar maple)

This commonly known native to the eastern United

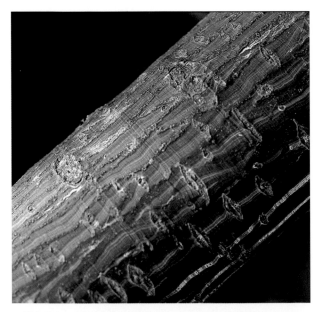

Striped maple bark in winter

> "Be like the sun and meadow, which are not in the least concerned about the coming winter."
> —*George Bernard Shaw*

States is often used to make maple syrup and maple sugar. Mature trees can become quite large and display brilliant shades of yellow or orange fall color. In New England and other parts of the Northeast, fall foliage is a main attraction, making up a good part of the tourism in this region of the country. In addition to the spectacular fall foliage colors, sugar maple also displays interesting bark. The rough, grayish brown, plated bark will develop thick, deep ridges with age and is very noticeable in the bare winter landscape.

Unlike the other maples mentioned, sugar maples will reach large sizes and must be sited in large open areas where they have plenty of room. They do not thrive in urban, polluted conditions, but perform best in rich, moist, well-drained soil and full sun. Sugar maples will also tolerate partial shade and are equally effective in a natural setting or in a cultivated garden environment. In hot, dry situations, their leaves will often get scorched from the heat of the sun. Sugar maple is best suited as a lawn tree, shade tree, and specimen in a naturalistic landscape. 'Green Mountain' has deep green leaves and yellow, orange, and sometimes red fall color. 'Legacy' is another superior variety with glossy, dark green foliage, dense growth habit, and excellent yellow, orange, or red fall color. Hardy from Zones 4–8.

{ *Aesculus parviflora*
Bottlebrush buckeye

Bottlebrush buckeye is one of the most magnificent flowering shrubs for summer and fall interest. In early summer, 12 in. long, white bristly flower spikes form and persist several weeks. The large, palm-shaped, dark green leaves provide a coarse texture during the summer and turn bright yellow in autumn. In late summer, fruit capsules form and disperse smooth, nonedible chestnut-like fruit.

But this reliable garden performer can also be interesting during the winter. The slender, gray, upright-growing stems create dense clumps that can grow 8–12 ft. tall with a potentially greater spread.

Bottlebrush buckeye is a low-maintenance shrub that prefers moist, well-drained, acidic soil with generous amounts of organic matter. It thrives in full sun or partial shade but will tolerate varying soil types and deep shade. Occasional selective pruning to thin out older stems will keep plants vigorous. Selective pruning can also be used to limit spreading and keep shrubs in scale.

Bottlebrush buckeye is very effective in a lawn area, as a specimen, and in a shade garden. Hardy from Zones 4–8; may grow in Zone 9 with proper siting.

{ *Amelanchier* spp.
Serviceberry, shadbush, juneberry

Serviceberry, also known as shadbush, is a large shrub or small tree that will enhance the winter landscape as it matures. This spring-flowering plant has small, white flowers and edible fruit in early summer. During the winter months, the smooth, silvery gray bark with noticeable silver streaks glistens in the winter landscape. Even the thinnest of branchlets has an attractive silver color enhanced by red, pointed buds. With age, mature specimens develop an upright, dense, and irregular growth pattern. These beautiful native American trees and shrubs will grace the landscape providing multiple seasons of interest.

Several important species are available yielding many superior varieties. The most common and reliable in cultivated landscapes are shadblow

The smooth, striped bark of *Amelanchier*

serviceberry (*Amelanchier canadensis*), apple service-berry (*Amelanchier* × *grandiflora*), and Allegheny serviceberry (*Amelanchier laevis*). A few excellent varieties that are suitable for the garden include 'Cumulus', which has a narrow, upright growth habit; 'Autumn Brilliance', with beautiful green summer foliage that will turn shades of brilliant red in the fall and has densely arranged gray stems; and 'Robin Hill', which offers pink flowers buds that unfold to pale pink or white flowers and has fall foliage that ranges from yellow to red.

Serviceberry is one of the most outstanding shrubs for edible fruit, which ripen early in the summer season (June). The sweet, succulent, blueberry-like fruit is adored by wildlife and humans alike. This multistemmed shrub has been known to stop me dead in my tracks so I can enjoy the sweet, sugary fruit. Serviceberry is ideal in small groupings or as a single specimen near a stream or pond. It is most effective when used as a naturalizing plant in a woodland setting. In its native habitat you will find this shrub growing in a shady, moist forest setting or in full sun along a windswept seashore landscape. Ideally serviceberry prefers full sun or partial shade and well-drained, moist, acidic soil. Leaf spots, rusts, and other diseases will sometimes bother serviceberry and may defoliate even mature specimens. However, these durable landscape shrubs will tolerate such pest problems. Serviceberry is generally hardy from Zones 4–8.

Betula spp.
Birch

What could be more identifiable in the winter landscape than the beautiful, white bark of birch? From New England to the Mid-Atlantic United States, birch is a well-known tree exhibiting showy, white bark that will catch the eye even from far away. Although they are variable, many birch species offer a smooth, milky white bark that shines in the winter landscape as the sunlight reflects off the trunks and branches. Often the white bark is accented by subtle hints of dark brown or black highlights. As with cherry trees, the young stems of birch also have noticeable lenticels, which are small glands irregularly arranged along the surface of the bark. These aesthetically pleasing lenticels are also functional since they allow gas exchange between plant cells and the environment. During the growing season, the dark green leaves offer a nice contrast to the white-colored bark. The leaves turn golden yellow in autumn, and in winter the white branches and trunks are fully revealed. In addition to bark interest, odd-looking male flowers called catkins will form at the tips of the branches. The catkins are long, thin, greenish brown flowers usually reaching several inches long that are displayed prominently in the winter.

The famous American poet Robert Frost wrote fondly about birch trees, and it is not too difficult to understand why: birch offers a certain aesthetic quality that inspires us unlike any tree in the winter landscape. In the dormant landscape as the bare, white stems are revealed, these magnificent trees become the

The distinctive white bark of birch

focal point of the garden. In essence, birch is nature's poetry, always offering an unmistakable presence to be admired and respected. They are one of the most identifiable, signature trees of New England and cold northern climates.

Birch does require a specific climate and growing conditions to thrive. Many species of birch are susceptible to damaging insect infestations. The worst of these pests are bronze birch borer and leaf miner. Borers will tunnel their way into the stems and trunk of a birch tree and can ultimately kill the tree if left untreated. Leaf miners, as their name suggests, tunnel their way into the leaves of the tree, causing an irregular tunneling pattern on individual leaves. This often results in cosmetic damage to the leaves, but in severe cases trees will defoliate, causing significant stress. Both of these pest problems can be treated, and you

should consult your local county extension service for advice. The species of birch most susceptible to these pests is European birch (*Betula pendula*) and gray birch (*Betula populifolia*).

Birch is typically considered a tree that is best suited for colder, northern climates; however, there are several species that will tolerate warm, humid climates as well. Birches like moist, well-drained soil, full sun or partial shade, and they perform particularly well in a woodland setting. In general, most of the birches discussed in this section are medium in size (approximately 40 ft.), but river birch (*Betula nigra*) can get considerably larger.

The epitome of white-barked birches is paper birch (*Betula papyrifera*), also called canoe birch because it was often used by Native Americans to make canoes and other wood products. This birch offers a soft wood that can readily be carved or sculpted. Paper birch received its name from the exquisite, chalky white bark that peels off like sheets of paper. In older trees the white bark is often highlighted by streaks of black, corky bark. This medium-sized tree sparkles in the winter sun against a dark evergreen background or a bright blue sky. One of the most widely distributed birches in North America. Hardy from Zones 2–7.

Another white-bark birch that is striking in the winter landscape is the Himalayan birch (*Betula utilis* var. *jacquemontii*). This medium-sized tree has an ultrasmooth, pure white bark that is among the most beautiful of any winter landscape tree. Although there have been some reports of this species being particularly susceptible to bronze birch borer, it will perform

The peeling bark of paper birch

Betula papyrifera in the landscape

admirably if sited correctly and provided adequate moisture. Himalayan birch is undoubtedly the whitest of the white-barked birches. It can be used as a single specimen in a lawn or in a small grouping in a partially shaded woodland. Hardy from Zones 5–7.

The whitespire birch (*Betula platyphylla* 'Whitespire') is a pest-resistant birch offering glossy green leaves during the summer that change to yellow in fall. In the winter, the beautiful chalky white bark becomes the highlight of the landscape. The bark does not exfoliate like many other birch species. 'Whitespire' is heat and drought tolerant and is very useful as a

specimen or in small groupings. Hardy from Zones 4–7.

Probably the most durable of all birch species is the river birch (*Betula nigra*). This widespread species is native to the United States from the Northeast to the South and parts of the Midwest. It is extremely tolerant of poorly drained soils, heat, humidity, and, most important, pests. Naturally occurring specimens of river birch are often found growing along streams and rivers, where there are very moist, silty soils.

There is quite a bit of variation among this species in relation to bark color, but most often this species has

River birch has flaking bark with tones of white, cinnamon, and gray.

Smooth, peeling bark of Heritage birch

Vincent A. Simeone

a cinnamon to creamy brown flaking bark that darkens with age. However, a very well-known variety called Heritage ('Cully') is an improved variety featuring creamy white bark with salmon tones—it is quite spectacular in the landscape. This birch typically gets quite large and is often used as a shade tree or lawn tree. But, because of the dramatic bark, ease of culture, and availability, it is one if the best birches for the winter garden. Heritage birch is a fast-growing variety that will establish quickly in the garden.

In general, birches are effective as a single specimen or in groupings in a cultivated or natural landscape. Birch is undoubtedly one of the most dramatic trees for bark interest. Whether you choose a single-stem or clump birch, which has three or more main trunks, it is hard to rival these picturesque trees. For the gardener strolling through the winter landscape, birch is like a beacon of bright light shining amongst the starkness of winter.

{ *Carpinus betulus*
European hornbeam

European hornbeam is a European hardwood species that is closely related to birch. Hornbeam is also referred to as ironwood or musclewood because of the smooth, steel gray sinuous bark that is especially interesting on older specimens. Young trees start off pyramidal but, once established, will develop into wide-spreading, majestic trees. This slow- to medium-growing tree adds great character to the landscape. It can be used as a single specimen or in groupings. In addition, it is often trained as a formal hedge, especially in Europe. The cultivated variety 'Fastigiata' is noticeably oval and upright, making it more suitable for garden areas with limited room. 'Fastigiata' can grow 40 ft. or more in height with half the spread. There is also an American native hornbeam (*Carpinus caroliniana*) that is typically

Carpinus betulus 'Fastigiata' in its natural form

Carpinus betulus hedge surrounding a gazebo in winter

found in natural woodland settings, but its European counterpart is more commercially available.

Like birch, hornbeam prefers moist, well-drained soil and full sun but is remarkably tolerant of poor soils, drought, and pollution. European hornbeam is hardy from Zones 5–7 but will grow in Zone 4 with protection.

{ *Clethra barbinervis* Japanese clethra

In addition to larger trees, many small- to medium-sized trees and shrubs will exhibit outstanding bark interest year-round. Japanese clethra (*Clethra barbinervis*) is a close relative to the shrubby, native summersweet clethra, (*Clethra alnifolia*), but it grows considerably taller. It is especially interesting in winter, displaying smooth, multicolored bark. The exfoliating bark displays shades of gray, beige, and rich brown, which contrast well in the winter landscape. Although this is a four-season characteristic, the bark is most noticeable during the winter months, as it shows up nicely against the background of evergreens. In addition to the beautiful bark, Japanese clethra also offers spikes of white flowers in early summer and lush, green leaves that turn red or maroon in autumn. After flowering, the brown fruit clusters develop and will persist into the winter season.

Japanese clethra grows best in moist, organic, well-drained soil and full sun or partial shade. It prefers to be sheltered from intense wind and other harshly exposed conditions. Gardeners must be patient since Japanese clethra requires a few years to establish in the landscape.

Smooth bark on Japanese clethra

This upright, multistemmed, large shrub or small tree can reach 15–20 ft. in height, making it suitable as a small specimen for a residential landscape. It can be used in a front yard in a similar manner as dogwood, crabapple, or flowering cherry. Hardy from Zones 5–7.

{ *Cornus* spp. Dogwood

Shrub dogwoods

Although dogwoods are considered among the elite of flowering trees for the home garden, there are several species that will offer a shrubby habit. These shrubby dogwoods can exhibit fine winter interest and are quite effective in groupings or mass plantings. Unlike the tree type dogwood species, shrub dogwoods display unusual, creamy white, flat-topped flowers in spring and summer. In addition, several species are well known for their colorful stems that will warm up a cold winter landscape.

The red twig dogwood (*Cornus sericea*), also known as redosier dogwood, has brilliant bloodred stems during the late autumn and winter months. While there are several related species that are also suited for the garden setting, redosier dogwood is the most common and most available in the horticultural industry. During the growing season, this shrub has a generic, leafy appearance. But upon the onset of cooler weather, falling leaves give way to deep red stems that ripen like an apple on a tree. These red stems are most evident against a blanket of freshly fallen snow or a contrasting background. The stem color is most vibrant on younger stems; therefore, an ongoing pruning program will ensure a new crop of brightly colored stems each year. The best way to encourage new stems is to selectively remove older stems every few years. These stems should be pruned at the base of the shrub while the plant is dormant in late winter or early spring. In addition to displaying a colorful show in the garden, branches can be harvested for holiday decorations as well. Although this shrub is primarily grown for its red stems, there are also several selections that offer yellow or orangey red winter color. 'Flaviramea' is a variety with bright yellow stems. Using both the red twig and yellow twig varieties in groupings together can be very effective. 'Winter Flame' is a relatively new variety with orangey yellow stems with pink or red accents that is also very striking in the landscape. These shrubby dogwoods prefer full sun and moist, well-drained soil for best performance. Plants can spread 10 ft. or more and will reach heights of 6 ft. or more, so these shrubs should be given plenty of room in the garden. *C. sericea* is hardy from Zones 2–7, but 'Winter Flame' is hardy from Zones 4–7.

The red stems of redosier dogwood

Yellow twig dogwood, *C. sericea* 'Flaviramea', (left) and red twig dogwood, *C. sericea,* in winter

Kousa dogwood covered by a blanket of snow

Tree type dogwoods

There are several species of dogwood that develop into small trees and can also add great interest to the winter landscape. One species of dogwood that one would least likely expect to exhibit winter interest is the American dogwood (*Cornus florida*). Flowering dogwoods have long been regarded as one of the great American native trees because of its showy white or pink spring blossoms. Many of us have fond memories growing up admiring the neighborhood dogwood trees that bloomed consistently each spring. Both the American dogwood and kousa dogwood (*Cornus kousa*) offer flowers with four showy bracts that are rivaled by few flowering trees. American dogwood blooms before leaves emerge in mid spring, while kousa dogwood blooms after the leaves have unfolded about three weeks later. In addition, these two species offer interesting fall fruit and outstanding reddish purple fall foliage color. But while these reliable trees are best known for their flowers, they also can offer interesting bark, stem, and growth characteristics that can be quite handsome in the winter.

The American dogwood matures into a dense, rounded tree that will eventually develop a rough, gray bark resembling alligator skin. The bark develops a coarse texture while the smooth, gray, rounded flower buds provide a subtle but interesting display. In contrast, its Asian counterpart, kousa dogwood (*Cornus kousa*), exhibits a beautiful flaking bark that displays shades of tan, gray, and brown. This multicolored, exfoliating bark has a camouflage appearance that is most prominent in the winter. This is especial-

The exfoliating bark of kousa dogwood

These garden favorites are excellent when used as a single specimen in a front lawn or in small groupings as part of a woodland planting. Hardy from Zones 5–7.

{ *Halesia tetraptera*
Carolina silverbell

This medium-sized tree can be a delightful addition to any garden and is best known for its silvery white bell-shaped flowers in spring. It is also quite noticeable during the winter months with vertical fissures of gray, brown, and black that form into plates on the main trunks. The younger stems are also gray brown with light streaks but are smoother than the older branches. Established trees will eventually form a rounded growth habit reaching 30 ft. or more high with an equal spread.

This often-overlooked tree is native to the southeastern United States and, while adaptable to many landscape situations, it thrives in well-drained, acidic, moist soils and full sun or partial shade. Silverbell is ideal as a single specimen or in a woodland setting in a sheltered area of the garden. Hardy from Zones 4–8 and possibly 9 with specific siting.

{ *Heptacodium miconioides*
Seven-son flower

This extraordinary Asian species is one of the most delightful large shrubs for the gardener who wants to try something unique. Although this somewhat obscure species is considered a four-season plant, it is undoubtedly at its best in the autumn and winter seasons.

ly true on older trees that develop thick, strong trunks and branches. The picturesque growth habit and exfoliating bark of kousa dogwood is very noticeable in winter.

Although American dogwood is known to be susceptible to several diseases such as dogwood anthracnose, it will be less likely to fall prey to these diseases if sited correctly in partially shaded areas of the garden with plenty of air circulation. Trees sited in dense shade are typically more susceptible to anthracnose and other pests. Kousa dogwood will perform well in full sun or partial shade and is quite resistant to dogwood anthracnose. Both dogwood species perform best in moist, acidic, well-drained soil with generous amounts of organic matter.

Smooth, light *Heptacodium* bark

months. The brown or gray bark exfoliates, unveiling a lighter underbark. This beautiful contrast is most noticeable while the plant is dormant.

Seven-son flower is best when used as a single specimen or in a small grouping. It can be trained as a small tree and will grow 12–15 ft. tall. While adaptable, seven-son flower performs best in moist, well-drained soil and full sun. Hardy from Zones 4–8.

Hydrangea quercifolia { Oakleaf hydrangea

Although hydrangeas are thought of as summer-blooming garden favorites, this extraordinary species also provides winter interest. Oakleaf hydrangea is a four-season shrub offering interesting leaves; large, white, cone-shaped summer flowers; brilliant red or maroon fall foliage; and beautiful, flaking bark in winter.

During the spring, unusual coarsely textured leaves that resemble the leaves of an oak tree unfurl and turn deep crimson to purple in the fall. The white, pyramidal flowers emerge in early to midsummer and change to pink as they age. But probably this flowering shrub's best attribute is the smooth, rich, cinnamon brown, peeling bark that develops on established plants. This attribute really stands out in the stark winter landscape when the bare stems are exposed. Dried flowers will often persist into the winter as well. Oakleaf hydrangea displays a dense, mounded growth habit that ranges from 4–8 ft. in height and spread.

Oakleaf hydrangea is a low-maintenance shrub that is quite adaptable in the landscape. It tolerates poor

Lush, green leaves cover the shrub in summer followed by small, creamy white flowers late in the season. After the flowers fade, clusters of deep red calyces are revealed, which are appendages that surround the flower. This aesthetically pleasing effect is interesting during the late summer and autumn. The smooth, flaking bark and strong, upright habit is appealing all year and is highlighted during the winter

soils and shade but thrives in moist, well-drained soil and full sun or partial shade. Oakleaf hydrangea is one of the more drought-tolerant and pest-resistant hydrangea species available. Selective pruning to remove older, unproductive stems can be done in late winter or early spring, while the plants are still dormant.

This multifaceted shrub is very functional in a mass planting, woodland garden, and along the foundation of the house. Below is a list of a few choice varieties ideal for the home landscape. Hardy from Zones 5–9.

NOTABLE VARIETIES

'Alice'. A large-growing and vigorous form with white flowers reaching 12 in. or more in length. This plant needs room and should only be used if given adequate space to grow. Large specimens will develop a large mass of thick branches with peeling bark in winter.

'Pee Wee'. A delightful little shrub with small, white flowers. Ideal for the home landscape.

'Sikes Dwarf'. Another compact selection with an upright, densely branched growth habit.

'Snow Queen'. A reliable performer growing to 6 ft. tall and wide. The large, white flowers and bronzy red fall foliage make this plant very desirable in the landscape.

'Snowflake'. A very unusual selection, with double white flowers exhibiting a lacy appearance. The large, heavy flowers droop off each branch in a graceful, weeping fashion. The flowers will change to pink in the fall and will usually persist into winter. The flowers are particularly interesting in dried flower arrangements.

{ *Lagerstroemia indica*
Crape myrtle

Crape myrtle has earned a reputation as a colorful, floriferous large shrub or small tree during the summer season. It is found extensively in gardens in the southeastern United States, where it is used in many landscape situations. It displays showy, papery flowers that range from white to pink to deep red. The flowers will often persist into fall. In addition to its summer and autumn attributes, this fast-growing shrub also displays impressive ornamental characteristics in the winter months, when the smooth, multicolored bark is at its best. As the outer layer of bark flakes off the trunk, shades of brown, beige, or gray are exposed. Because of crape myrtle's upright habit, smooth bark texture, and striking color, established specimens provide a strong presence in the landscape.

Crape myrtle is a very adaptable shrub, thriving in hot, sunny locations in the garden. It thrives in moist, well-drained soils but is very tolerant of poor, dry soils. Winter fertilization will help increase flower production and vigor. If significant pruning is needed, selective pruning while the plant is dormant in late winter is recommended. Otherwise, light pruning right after bloom time can be done during the growing season. To train taller-growing crape myrtle varieties as small trees, prune off any young, spindly or thin branches from the lower part of the plant, leaving several mature main stems.

Crape myrtle is hardy from Zones 6–9 but does benefit from a sheltered location in colder climates. A light layer of mulch or pine straw will also help to

Crape myrtle bark

'Acoma'. A semi-dwarf selection growing 5–10 ft. high and wide with white flowers and light gray bark.

'Hopi'. This shrubby crape myrtle will produce light pink flowers and variations of brown/gray bark.

'Lipan'. An interesting variety with lavender flowers and beige/white bark. This is an intermediate form that can grow 15–20 ft.

'Natchez'. A beautiful, large-growing variety with pure white flowers and cinnamon brown bark. Excellent as a small tree for a home landscape provided adequate room is available.

'Tuscarora'. Attractive dark coral pink flowers are a nice contrast to the light brown, smooth bark. This variety can get large and is easily trained as a small tree.

In addition to these varieties, there is a larger growing species, *Lagerstroemia faurei*, which has an exquisite vase-shaped growth habit and stunning reddish brown bark. The bark interest is equal to that of stewartia. An outstanding medium-sized tree for the home garden, 'Fantasy' is a popular, fast-growing variety with exceptional bark interest.

protect the roots from fluctuating soil temperature and varying degrees of moisture.

Crape myrtle is a multipurpose plant and can be used as a small specimen tree or in groupings. It is important to decide which type of crape myrtle you want since there are many varieties to choose from.

Below is a listing of some good varieties for good bark interest.

{ *Ostrya virginiana*
American hophornbeam

The American hophornbeam is a birch relative and American native with multiple seasons of interest. While the dark green summer leaves have a relatively generic appearance, the dense, rounded habit and rough, grayish brown shaggy bark are very distinctive in the winter landscape. In addition, small male flowers (catkins) in groups of three are abundant on the tips of the branches all winter. The distinctive, papery fruit cluster resembles the fruit of hops, thus the name hophornbeam. Fruit develop in summer and will often persist into much of the fall and winter.

Hophornbeam is a hard-wooded, slow-growing tree maturing to 30–40 ft. tall with a slightly smaller spread. It prefers moist, well-drained soil but will tolerate dry, rocky soils. Full sun or partial shade is best for this woodland tree. Hophornbeam is an excellent tree for a shady part of the garden. It can be used as a small specimen in a lawn area or in small groupings. Hardy from Zones 3–9.

Parrotia persica
Persian parrotia

Persian parrotia is one of the most amazing medium-sized trees available for the winter landscape. As it develops, so will your admiration for this outstanding, four-season plant. Like a fine wine, parrotia improves with age. Persian parrotia is native to Iran and is in the same family as witch hazel. As the tree matures, it develops twisted, sinuous branches and an upright, spreading growth habit. One special feature of parrotia is the exquisite exfoliating bark, displaying shades of tan, green, gray, and brown. This ornamental characteristic is a showstopper in the winter.

Because of its natural beauty, parrotia should be used as a specimen plant and can easily function as a focal point in the landscape. In addition to beautiful bark and growth habit, parrotia also offers beau-

Parrotia has a beautiful, irregular growth pattern and exfoliating bark

tiful lustrous green foliage that turns brilliant shades of yellow, orange, and maroon in the fall. The peculiar, frilly, reddish maroon flowers in early spring, although subtle, are an added feature.

Parrotia should be grown in moist, well-drained soils in full sun or partial shade. It adapts remarkably well to various soil types and environmental conditions, including heat, humidity, drought and cold. Parrotia tends to be fast growing at youth and slower growing as it matures and can easily grow to 20–30 ft. high and wide. This tree is hardy from Zones 4–8. It is truly one of the most extraordinary exotic trees, which is why it has been featured on the cover of this book.

{ *Phellodendron amurense* Amur corktree

The amur corktree has earned its name from its unusually corky, fissured bark. The soft, spongy surface of the bark resembles the cork material used to manufacture many cork products. However, true cork is actually harvested from an oak native to southern Europe. While the corky bark is one of several ornamental features, it is the most noticeable characteristic during the winter when the tree is leafless. As corktree matures, it becomes quite upright, spreading and picturesque. This Asian species also has lustrous green leaves during the summer months and golden yellow fall color.

Corktree is one of the toughest trees in the landscape, tolerating poor soils, varying soil pH, drought, and other adverse conditions. However, corktree does best in full sun and well-drained, moist soils. Like many other shade trees, corktree should be used as a specimen plant or in a lawn setting. It is hardy from Zones 4–7 and will grow 30–40 ft. high and wide.

{ *Physocarpus opulifolius* Common ninebark

This American native naturally grows from Quebec, Canada, to the eastern and midwestern United States. This fast-growing ornamental shrub offers white or light pink flowers in mid to late spring and medium green leaves in the summer. In the winter, the older stems of mature specimens are quite noticeable, displaying peeling sheets of brown bark.

Ninebark is a very adaptable shrub, tolerating various soil types and light conditions. It thrives in full sun or partial shade and moist, well-drained soil. Pruning should be kept to a minimum in order to encourage the peeling bark interest on mature branches. If left unpruned, this shrub can reach 10 ft. tall with a similar spread.

Ninebark can be effective as mass plantings, screens, or as a single specimen. For summer foliage interest, there are several varieties that offer colored leaves. 'Dart's Gold' has bright yellow leaves that fade to yellow-green with age. 'Diablo' has reddish maroon summer foliage that is most colorful on young stems. It is an extremely cold-hardy plant, growing in Zones 2–7.

{ *Prunus* spp. Ornamental cherry

While there are species of cherry that are appreciated for their edible fruit, there are numerous cherries that are grown for their ornamental characteristics—showy spring flowers, ornamental foliage, and beautiful textured bark. This bark can be rather striking in the winter.

Cherry bark can offer a diverse selection of color and texture, but there are several common and consistent characteristics. One main characteristic is an irregular pattern of horizontally arranged lenticels, which are noticeable glands on the surface of the bark. These rough, woody lenticels provide an interesting contrast to the smooth bark of the tree. Bark color on ornamental cherries can range from tan to gray-brown to dark brown, depending on the species. Although it is difficult to believe that a flowering tree can be appreciated during the winter months, cherries are one of the most "stand out" trees in the winter landscape because of their bark. Even hiking through the forest, nature lovers can easily identify cherry trees growing in the wild.

In general, cherries perform best in moist, well-drained, acidic soil and full sun or partial shade. They are susceptible to various insects and diseases, so careful monitoring is essential to ensure trees remain healthy.

Siting of these ornamental trees is important to fully appreciate their interesting form and texture. Flowering cherries are most effective when used as a single specimen, in small groupings, or in larger mass plantings. The mass plantings of ornamental cherries in Washington, D.C., is a breathtaking sight to behold early in the spring season.

While there are many species and varieties of flowering cherries, three very common species of flowering cherries are Oriental cherry (*Prunus serrulata*), weeping Higan cherry (*Prunus subhirtella* 'Pendula'), and Yoshino cherry (*Prunus* x *yedoensis*). While these three

Horizontal lenticels on cherry bark .

Cherry in the winter landscape

species are spectacular in the landscape, here are a few other lesser known and choice garden favorites suited for the home landscape.

Prunus x *incamp* 'Okame' ('Okame' cherry)

This upright, medium-sized cherry offers rosy pink, delicate, single flowers as early as March if temperatures are mild. 'Okame' also has small, dark green leaves that turn deep orange or bronzy red during the autumn. However, 'Okame' cherry is also quite noticeable in the winter months, showing off its upright vase-shaped growth habit and ornamental dark, reddish brown bark with gray lenticels.

'Okame' cherry grows 20–30 ft. high with a similar spread and is hardy from Zones 6–8. It is ideal as a single specimen or in small groupings in areas of the garden where winter interest and early spring color is desired. A very useful tree near a patio or in a lawn area to cast some shade.

Prunus 'Hally Jolivette' ('Hally Jolivette' cherry)

The 'Hally Jolivette' cherry is a small flowering cherry that is most suitable for gardens with limited space. It is a fine-textured tree that can also develop a multi-stemmed, shrublike appearance. The flowers emerge in spring, light pink or nearly white, often with deep pink centers, and last for several weeks. The small delicate leaves will change to bronzy red in the fall. Once the leaves fall in the autumn, the light grayish tan stems and branches are uncovered. The bark has a light tan or grayish color that is quite noticeable in winter.

'Hally Jolivette' prefers full sun or partial shade and moist, well-drained soil. Pruning should be kept to a minimum since this tree will not grow very large, but occasional selective pruning to keep plants tidy may be desired. The growth habit commonly remains dense and mounded, and 'Hally Jolivette' can be grown as a single-stem tree or mulitstemmed large shrub. This fine cherry will grow to 15 ft. tall and is hardy from Zones 5–7.

Prunus mume (Japanese apricot)

Japanese apricot is a handsome ornamental flowering tree that reaches 20 ft. tall with a dense, rounded growth habit. The fragrant, single or double showy flowers are borne on shiny green stems and range from white, pink, rose, or red as early as midwinter and continuing through early spring. This delightful, fast-

The striking flowers of 'Peggy Clarke'

growing, small, flowering tree is a favorite in Japan, where it is highly cultivated. 'Peggy Clarke' is an excellent double-flowering, deep rose pink variety. The popularity of this plant in America was the result of the tireless efforts of the late J. C. Raulston, a famed horticulturist from North Carolina State University.

Like most cherries, Japanese apricot prefers moist, well-drained soil and full sun or partial shade. Hardy from Zones 6–9. In addition to the flowering apricot, the blireana plum (*Prunus* x *blireana*) offers pink, double flowers in early spring and reddish purple foliage that fades to green in the summer.

Salix matsudana
Hankow willow

Willows are available in many shapes and sizes, from shrubby pussy willows to large weeping willows. In addition to soft, fuzzy flowers and graceful, pendulous branching habits, several species and varieties also provide bark interest during the winter. In fact, two varieties of the hankow willow are specifically grown for such bark interest. 'Golden Curls' is a tall shrub or small tree and has golden, curly stems that twist and weep toward the ground. The striking golden color is rather showy during the winter months, especially on young plants. 'Scarlet Curls' has a similar habit, but young stems are scarlet and older branches remain golden yellow to brown.

Hankow willow prefers moist soils but will adapt to drier conditions as well. Willows are fast growing and will grow several feet in one year, if healthy. A regular pruning program to cut shrubs low to the ground every few years will encourage the brightly colored stems. This type of severe pruning in early spring will also encourage a shrubby, dense habit. The stems can effectively be used in an arrangement or decorative vase. Hardy from Zones 5–8.

Stephanandra incisa
Cutleaf stephanandra

This graceful, mounded flowering shrub is best known for spring and summer interest, but it can also provide subtle but effective winter interest. Stephanandra has densely intertwined branches that form a thick cluster. The stem color during the winter is light tan or brown and can be rather interesting.

The small, finely cut leaves emerge a reddish bronze color in spring before changing to medium green during the summer. The leaves eventually change to shades of yellow, orange, and sometimes red in the fall. In spring, small clusters of white flowers open and will persist for a few weeks.

Stephanandra is a medium- to fast-growing shrub growing 4–8 ft. high with an equal spread. It adapts well to many different landscape situations but thrives in moist, well-drained, acidic soil. Plants perform best when sited in full sun or partial shade. Regular pruning is not often needed because of this shrub's dense, naturally cascading branching habit.

Stephanandra is ideal in mass plantings, small groupings, as an informal hedge, and even suitable as a screening plant due to its dense habit. Hardy from

Stephanandra incisa stems in winter

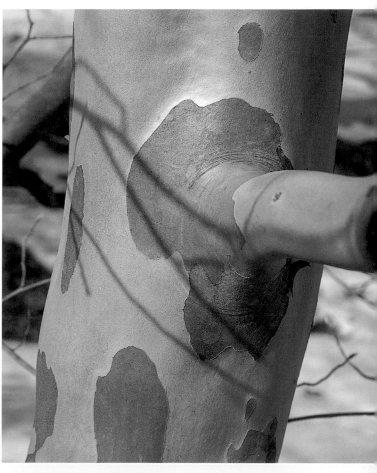

Multicolored bark of stewartia

Zones 4–7 but may also grow in Zone 8 if sited correctly in a cool, shaded area of the garden.

'Crispa' is a more compact variety with a low, spreading habit. This dwarf form will reach 2–3 ft. high with a slightly wider spread. It is very effective as a groundcover, mass planting, and edging plant.

{ *Stewartia pseudocamellia*
Japanese stewartia

Of all of the beautiful trees with outstanding bark characteristics, stewartia is clearly head and shoulders above most. This magnificent flowering tree is a four-season plant with white blooms in summer, intense red or orange fall foliage color, and lovely, multicolored bark. In early to mid summer, the flower buds emerge and look like large pearls before opening to pure white flowers with bright yellow centers. Flowers will continue for several weeks throughout the summer season. In the fall, the dark green foliage changes to brilliant shades of yellow,

Smooth trunk of stewartia

Stewartia should be sited in a highly visible area of the garden. It is a quintessential specimen tree that is suitable for a woodland garden, lawn area, or as a companion plant to rhododendrons, azaleas, and other flowering shrubs. There are several other worthy species of stewartia for the garden, all of which will impress the avid gardener. I have never met a stewartia I did not like. Hardy from Zones 4–7 but needs protection in Zone 4.

{ *Syringa reticulata*
Japanese tree lilac

Although it may be hard to believe, even lilacs can have winter interest. These beloved spring-flowering shrubs can offer more than just pretty blooms. But Japanese tree lilac is much different than the common lilac, which is well known for its sweetly fragrant white, purple, or pink flowers. Japanese tree lilac is an upright, small to medium tree that displays dark brown bark and a vase-shaped growth habit. The bark has noticeable lenticels and resembles that of cherry bark in winter. The bark is very dark and will contrast nicely against a snowy background.

During the late spring and early summer, plumes of white, fragrant flowers emerge and will persist for several weeks. Leaves will remain dark green all summer but do not develop striking fall color.

Japanese tree lilac prefers full sun, although it is tolerant of partial shade. It also prefers moist, well-drained soil but is adaptable to varying degrees of soil pH. Japanese tree lilac can be vulnerable to common lilac pests and my need some maintenance. Japanese tree lilac is ideal as a single specimen tree, in groupings, and has even been used as a street tree. Hardy from Zones 3–7.

orange, red, and maroon, also lasting for several weeks. But the most spectacular asset of this tree is the smooth, peeling bark that exhibits shades of tan, brown, gray, and beige all year. In winter, stewartia lights up the landscape with its extraordinarily colorful trunk and stems.

Stewartia is also a care-free tree ideal for the residential garden. It will grow 20–30 ft. tall and half that in width. Stewartia is a pest-free plant that prefers full sun or partial shade and well-drained, acidic, moist soil. Although it needs some time to establish, this choice specimen tree is well worth the wait. It has a medium to slow growth rate and will eventually develop into a dense tree with an oval to pyramidal growth habit.

Flowers in Winter?
Small Miracles Can Happen
Everyday in the Winter Garden

Flowers are most often associated with spring and summer as the sun warms the soil and highlights the colorful blossoms of our most beloved garden plants. Flowers are the single most identifiable aesthetic characteristic of a plant because they attract our eye with their bright, showy colors. But flowers do not develop exclusively during the spring and summer growing season. Although difficult to imagine, some trees and shrubs bloom in the colder weather from late autumn to late winter, when temperatures are cool and crisp. These resilient flowers are an eye-opening reminder that choice landscape plants are a gift to be appreciated throughout the year!

Unusual shrubs such as wintersweet, witch hazel, and flowering quince adorn their branches with showy and often fragrant flowers when the cool weather seems to be rather unforgiving. These flowers are adapted to endure the harsh elements that winter and early spring often present to them. For

"Flowers are beautiful hieroglyphics of nature, with which she indicates how much she loves us."
—*Johann Wolfgang von Goethe*

example, when a witch hazel blooms in mid to late winter, the curly, straplike flowers will unfold on a clear winter's day, basking in the warmth off the sun. But on days when the temperatures are exceptionally chilly, windy and dark, the flower petals will fold up tight, protected from the elements.

This section highlights some of the best landscape plants for winter and early spring flowering interest. These are shrubs and trees that are ideal to view from a window or a patio so they can be enjoyed from indoors as well as outdoors. These winter gems bring the garden to life with their interesting and sometimes fragrant flowers.

{ *Chaenomeles speciosa*
Common flowering quince

Flowering quince has been cultivated for centuries and is prized for its late-winter and early spring flowers. The flowers vary from white to pink to deep red in late winter and persist until mid-spring. Flowers are arranged in clusters along the interior of the shrub. In addition, smooth, fragrant apple-like fruit ripen in the fall and persist into winter, adding ornamental interest. Fruit can be harvested for decorative purposes or cooked and used to make preserves and jellies.

The twigs of flowering quince are spiny and should to be handled very carefully. Shrubs form a mass of thin, irregular-growing branches reaching 6–8 ft. high

Quince flowers in early spring

and wide. Flowering quince performs best in full sun and moist, well-drained, acidic soil but is extremely adaptable. Selective pruning can be done in early spring to remove old, unproductive branches.

Flowering quince is very effective as a barrier hedge and can also be used in groupings, mass plantings, and in shrub borders. Many gardeners plant it in the garden for early spring interest and to harvest the fruit in the fall. Zones 4–9.

NOTABLE VARIETIES

'Apple Blossom'. Large, 2 in. diameter pale pink flowers.

'Cameo'. Peachy pink double flowers in profusion.

'Toyo-Nishiki'. A unique selection with a combination of white, pink, and red flowers.

{ *Chimonanthus praecox*
Fragrant wintersweet

This fragrant winter-blooming shrub will display small, cup-shaped flowers in winter while most plants lie dormant. The small, yellow flowers with deep reddish centers appear as early as December or January and may continue through February or March in southern climates, depending on the winter temperatures. The tall, upright habit will form a large shrub or small tree reaching 10–15 ft. The dark green, sharply pointed, rough-textured summer leaves feel like sandpaper and will turn greenish yellow in the autumn.

Wintersweet is a relatively easy plant to grow and will adapt to varying types of soil texture. This flowering shrub prefers moist, well-drained soil and full sun or partial shade. In northern climates, shrubs should be sited in a protected area of the garden. Regular selective pruning to remove older, less productive stems should be done when the plant is dormant.

Wintersweet is effective as a small specimen or in groupings and is especially useful when placed in an area of the garden where the delightful fragrance can be enjoyed. Dormant branches can also be cut and forced into flower indoors. Hardy from Zones 6–9.

{ *Cornus mas*
Cornelian cherry

This early-flowering tree is remarkably adaptable and displays several unique ornamental characteristics. In late winter or early spring, small bouquets of yellow flowers will open and persist for several weeks. The glossy green leaves and cherry-red fruit in summer are also very attractive. But during the winter months this small- to medium-sized tree is very effective exhibiting a rough, exfoliating, and rich brown bark. The thin, green stems and rounded flower buds also add subtle interest. Cornelian cherry will grow 20–25 ft. tall with a slightly smaller spread.

Wintersweet flowers in the winter sun

Bright yellow Cornelian cherry blooms in late winter

Cornelian cherry is a tough landscape tree, tolerating poor soils and exposed sites, but it thrives in moist, well-drained soil and full sun or partial shade. It can be very useful as a single specimen, in raised planters or in small groupings. Hardy from Zones 4–7 but will tolerate Zone 8 with specific siting.

{ *Corylopsis pauciflora* Buttercup winterhazel

Buttercup winterhazel is a fine-textured, spreading shrub suitable for the home landscape. Winterhazel offers a profuse show of delicate yellow, fragrant flowers in early spring that persist for several weeks.

Buttercup winterhazel will grow to 5 ft. high and will spread to 6–8 ft. This shrub is so dense it is difficult to see through even in the winter. After flowering, small, textured green leaves emerge for the summer and turn yellow in the fall.

Winterhazel thrives in moist, organic, acidic, well-drained, soil and full sun or partial shade. Pruning should be kept to a minimum, as excessive pruning will compromise the exquisite growth habit. Poorly developed plants can be selectively pruned in early spring to remove older or damaged stems, which will also encourage new spring growth.

Buttercup winterhazel is an excellent woodland shrub when used in masses or small groupings and can also be effective as a low screen or informal hedge. In general, winterhazel should be given ample room to spread. Hardy from Zones 6–8.

There are several larger-growing winterhazel species—including fragrant winterhazel (*Corylopsis*

Buttercup winterhazel in flower

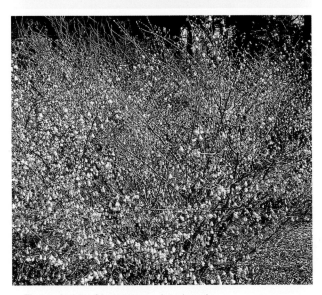
Dense habit of buttercup winterhazel

glabrescens) and spike winterhazel (*Corylopsis spicata*)—that are suited for larger landscapes with adequate room. Established plants can easily exceed 8–12 ft. wide with a similar height. The dangling, fragrant yellow flowers develop along irregular, crooked stems for a spectacular early-season display. The bare, brown stems offer an artistic branching pattern during the winter months. During the spring, dark green leaves develop and range from yellow green to golden yellow in the fall. Winterhazels are easy to grow and will perform best in moist shaded areas of the backyard. Winterhazel should receive infrequent pruning and be given adequate room to spread. Occasional selective pruning to remove older stems will keep plants vigorous. Winterhazel is effective in groupings, woodland gardens, as a screen, or as a single specimen.

Harry Lauder's walking stick stems with catkins

Corylus avellana 'Contorta'
Harry Lauder's walking stick

As mentioned earlier in this book, the birch family is well known for displaying interesting flowers called catkins. Filbert (*Corylus* spp.) is a birch relative that offers long, prominent catkins that dangle along each stem like holiday ornaments in winter and early spring.

Filbert can provide a unique and interesting effect during the winter. This odd-looking shrub forms a thick mass of twisted branches as it grows. It was discovered around 1863 in Frocester, Gloucestershire, England. Harry Lauder was one of Britain's most celebrated music hall comics/singers in the early twentieth century and is still one of Scotland's highest sell-

Male catkins

ing recording artists of all time. This shrub gained its name because one of Lauder's characters used a crooked hazelwood cane.

The combination of the irregular stems and the catkins make this multistemmed shrub a nice specimen plant. It will be a conversation piece in the garden even while dormant. The growth habit is mounded and the shrub can reach 8–10 ft. or more in height.

Harry Lauder's walking stick prefers well-drained, moist soil and full sun or partial shade. Pruning should be kept to a minimum to preserve the irregular, picturesque habit. Occasional thinning of older, weak stems or frequent removal of suckers from the base will maintain plant health and vigor. Harry Lauder's walking stick is a specialty plant and should be used as a specimen. It will most certainly be a focal point in any garden setting. Hardy from Zones 4–8.

Vincent A. Simeone

Spring heath in the landscape

{ *Erica carnea*
Spring heath

Spring heath is a close relative of rhododendrons and azaleas and is a very fine-textured groundcover. It has small, needlelike foliage and petite, bell-shaped flowers in late winter or early spring. The flowers range in color from white to pink or red, depending on the cultivated variety. The flowers line up along the tips of the stems en masse, providing a beautiful show. From a distance, theses ground huggers appear like undulating waves of green and pastel colors amongst the landscape. Unless temperatures are extreme, spring heath will bloom very early in the spring season to provide a hint of spring before most shrubs are blooming.

Like rhododendron, spring heath requires moist, very well-drained, acidic soil with generous amounts of organic matter. Since the fibrous roots are very shallow, a light layer of mulch (1-2 in.) is also beneficial to help keep the area around the soil cool and evenly moist. Spring heath thrives in full sun or partial shade along hills or raised flower beds.

Spring heath is ideal as a groundcover in mass plantings or groupings, rock gardens, or along a path where its fine texture can be enjoyed. There are many varieties available with various foliage and flower colors. Heather (*Calluna* spp.) is a very similar groundcover that will offer beautiful foliage during the winter as well and summer or autumn flowers. Hardy from Zones 5–7.

{ *Hamamelis* spp.
Witch hazel

Members of the witch hazel family offer very showy, unusual flowers during the winter and early spring season. The common witch hazel (*Hamamelis virginiana*) native to North America blooms in the autumn, and the popular winter-blooming Asian species and hybrids bloom in winter. Witch hazels' (*Hamamelis* spp.) best attribute is their thin, straplike flower petals that unfold in late winter. On very cold days the flowers will curl up and nearly close up to avoid damage from freezing temperatures. However, when the sun is at its strongest in the middle of the day, the warming effect will allow the flowers to open. In addition to showy flowers, some species and varieties will offer a pleasant fragrance. One added incentive to grow this shrub is that branches can be cut and forced into flower indoors. Witch hazel possesses a wide-spreading or vase-shaped growth habit and dark green, textured leaves that change to golden yellow, orange, and occasionally red in the autumn.

Witch hazels prefer moist, well-drained, rich, organic soil. Pruning should be kept to a minimum so that the naturally graceful growth habit will not be spoiled.

Witch hazel is one of a few flowering shrubs that have flowers that can withstand the cold, harsh elements of winter. Witch hazels are excellent winter shrubs that can be used effectively as a specimen plant or in small groupings. They should be sited in the garden where they can be viewed from a window in the house. Witch hazel is a wide-spreading, large shrub

Witch hazel blooming in the landscape

that reaches 10–15 ft. wide with an equal height. Because of this wide habit, poorly sited plants will eventually outgrow a confined area of the garden. When choosing a location for your witch hazel, remember to place it where it will have plenty of room to extend its long, spreading branches. Hardy from Zones 5–8.

Hamamelis mollis (Chinese witch hazel)

Chinese witch hazel has fragrant, bright yellow flowers with red centers. The flower petals are thin, curly,

> "The flowers of late winter and early spring occupy places in our hearts well out of proportion to their size".
> —*Gertrude S. Wister*

and straplike in appearance. The soft, fuzzy, dark green leaves display shades of yellow and orange in fall. The wide-spreading, layered growth habit of Chinese witch hazel is also quite interesting during the winter months when the branches are bare.

Hamamelis x *intermedia* (hybrid witch hazel)
This hybrid witch hazel is the most popular of all the witch hazel species. This garden favorite exhibits a strong, upright, vase-shaped habit that will also spread out in the garden. There are many garden varieties of this hybrid, and flowers range from bright yellow to orange and ruby red. The fall foliage color varies from year to year but typically displays shades of yellow, orange, and red.

Chinese witch hazel is not finicky and will adapt to a variety of soil types. It does perform best in moist, well-drained soil and full sun or partial shade. Witch hazel is a real garden treasure and will be the central attraction in a winter wonderland.

NOTABLE VARIETIES
'Arnold Promise'. A very popular variety with large, bright yellow flowers with red centers and effective fall color. Excellent in groupings or as a single specimen.

'Diane'. This form has striking brick red flowers, which are very prominent in the winter landscape, especially against a blanket of snow. This variety is truly spectacular when in full flower.

'Jelena'. One of my favorite selections, with large,

Chinese witch hazel in bloom

'Jelena' in flower

bright coppery orange flowers and superb orange-red fall color.

'Primavera'. Bright yellow, fragrant flowers are accented with rich red centers.

{ *Jasminum nudiflorum*
Winter jasmine

This prolific bloomer provides a welcomed display of delicate yellow flowers from mid to late winter into early spring. The small, trumpet-shaped blooms will sporadically open along older stems for several months. In addition, the mounded, cascading green stems will form a thick mat of growth reaching 4 ft. tall with twice the spread. In spring, small, glossy, dark green leaves unfold and remain until fall.

Winter jasmine is a low-growing shrub that will perform best in moist, well-drained soil and full sun or partial shade. It adapts to poor, infertile soils and is also drought tolerant. Straggly plants can easily be rejuvenated by severely pruning plants down to 6 in. early in spring. This type of pruning usually does not need to be done very often.

Winter jasmine is active in the garden when most shrubs are still sleeping. It is effective in groupings, mass plantings, or around the foundation of a house. Because of its cascading habit, winter jasmine is ideal along rock walls and slopes. This adaptable plant is cold hardy in Zones 6–10.

Vincent A. Simeone

Winter jasmine and Pickles the dog in the landscape

Winter jasmine flowers

{ *Lonicera fragrantissima*
Winter honeysuckle

Winter honeysuckle is a deciduous, medium-sized shrub that displays fragrant, creamy white flowers in late winter and early spring. The small, delicate, and numerous flowers line up along each stem and provide an extraordinarily fragrant display of flowers. The specific epithet, *fragrantissima*, describes the unusual intoxicatingly sweet fragrance of the blossoms. The genus was named after naturalist, alchemist, physician, and author of a famous 1578 text on herbs, Adam Lonitzer (1528–1586).

> "The seasons have just drifted by,
> Many moons have graced the sky,
> Whilst winter's honeysuckle bloom
> has filled the air with sweet perfume."
> —*Joyce Hensley*

Although a native of China, this multistemmed shrub is adaptable to a variety of environmental conditions in the United States. It will thrive in moist, well-drained, acidic soil but tolerates poor soils as well. Full sun or partial shade is best to develop masses of beautiful flowers in winter. Occasional selective pruning will encourage a vigorous, compact, and productive shrub. Winter honeysuckle is a carefree grower, and in certain areas of the country, such as Tennessee, it is considered an invasive exotic plant. Consult your local extension agency in your area to find out if this shrub is right for your garden.

Winter honeysuckle can reach 8–10 ft. tall with a similar spread. The smooth, dark green leaves will fall in unusually cold winters, but typically a portion of the foliage remains most of the winter. The rough-textured, light tan or gray bark on older stems is prominent in winter. It is an excellent choice near a walkway or garden path where the fragrance from the flowers can be enjoyed. Hardy from Zones 4–8.

{ *Salix* spp.
Pussy willow

Although some willows mentioned earlier in this book are known for their brightly colored stems in winter, there are also several species of willow that are admired for their soft, silky flowers in late winter. Pussy willows have a shrubby habit and offer soft, fuzzy male flowers, called catkins. These felt-textured flowers develop as the milder weather approaches, hinting that spring is on its way.

Like all willows, pussy willow prefers very moist soils and full sun or partial shade. It is fast growing, and gardeners interested in floral arranging can harvest branches to display in a vase. Pussy willows should be planted in areas of the garden where they will be well watered or located near streams and ponds where water is plentiful.

Although there are several species of pussy willow that are commercially available, goat willow (*Salix caprea*) and black pussy willow (*Salix melanostachys*)

Black pussy willow in flower

Goat willow in flower

are two worthwhile garden shrubs that can be used as cutback shrubs. Goat willow has soft, gray, silky flowers in early spring, while the black pussy willow has striking, fuzzy, black flowers. Both of these species remain shrubby and perform well in most landscape situations provided they have adequate moisture. Established plantings will also tolerate drier areas of the garden. Goat willow will grow from Zones 4–8, and black pussy willow will grow from Zones 4–7.

Stachyurus praecox

This unusual shrub is not a well-known garden plant, but it possesses a great deal of winter beauty. While the plant is dormant and leafless, long, slender flower clusters hang off each branch. In late winter and early spring, the flowers will elongate, ranging from 2–8 in. long and open to a pale yellow. The pendulous form of the abundant flowers is quite a sight. The multistemmed growth habit is graceful, reaching 6 ft. tall with a similar spread.

Stachyurus is a collector's plant and can be found in specialty mail-order nursery catalogs and retail nurseries. *Stachyurus* prefers moist, well-drained soil and will thrive in both full sun and partial shade.

Stachyurus is an excellent small specimen for a woodland garden or near a walkway where the unusual, dangling flowers can be enjoyed. Branches can also be harvested and used in floral arrangements along with other winter-blooming shrubs. Hardy from Zones 6–8 and should be sited in a cool, moist, shady area of the garden in warm climates.

'Dawn' viburnum in flower

'Dawn' viburnum displaying pink buds

Viburnum × *bodnatense* 'Dawn'
'Dawn' viburnum

This extremely sweet-smelling viburnum has an intoxicating fragrance when in bloom. 'Dawn' viburnum is one of the earliest flowering selections of viburnum. I have witnessed it in bloom as early as December and as late as May in the northeastern United States. The deep pink flower clusters will open sporadically through the late winter or early spring when temperatures are not exceedingly cold. The upright growth habit and coarse branches make this plant a bold fixture in the landscape. However, this shrub can become rather awkward and appear unkempt if left unpruned; therefore, it should be pruned regularly in late winter to remove older stems. This type of selective maintenance pruning will encourage vigorous and productive growth. Unpruned specimens can grow to 10 ft. or more high.

In addition to the colorful, fragrant flowers, 'Dawn' viburnum also has handsome, textured green leaves that turn a deep bronzy red to maroon in fall. 'Dawn' is excellent as a single specimen but can also be used in small groupings, informal hedges, and as a backdrop to smaller plantings. Cut branches can be brought indoors, and the flowers will quickly respond by opening and filling the house with its pleasant perfume.

The Fruits of Their Labor

Trees and shrubs can display beautiful, succulent fruit that develop in the late summer or fall season but remain even in the bitter cold of winter. These attractive fruit can provide a showy display of red, orange, or yellow even though the plant is dormant. In addition to aesthetic value, the fruit on some species can also provide a source of high protein food for birds and other garden creatures. While flowers can be quite attractive in the garden, the anticipation of the fruit developing from these flowers is equally thrilling. Here are a few good woody plant selections to add fruit interest to the winter landscape.

"And the fruits will outdo what the flowers have promised."

—*Francois de Malherbe*

{ *Aronia arbutifolia*
Red chokecherry

Red chokecherry is a multistemmed shrub with several seasons of interest. It offers small, showy clusters of white flowers in spring. These small bouquets develop into deep red, glossy fruit, which persist through fall and early winter. This is one of a few shrubs that bear nonedible fruit, which even birds will avoid due to their sour taste. The shiny, dark green foliage of chokecherry turns reddish maroon in fall and provides a nice contrast to the fruit.

Chokecherry is very adaptable to a variety of soil types but prefers well-drained, acidic soil with moderate moisture. It is also quite drought tolerant once established and will grow in hot, dry conditions, even near the seashore. Full sun is best for maximum flower and fruit production, but partial shade is also acceptable. Selective pruning to remove older, less productive stems can be done every few years to promote a continuous healthy crop of vigorous stems.

Chokecherry is an excellent choice for mass plantings, small groupings, foundation plantings, shade gardens, and it can be very effective near the seashore. Hardy from Zones 4–9.

'Brilliantissima' is a superior variety with exceptional red/crimson fall color, an abundance of flowers, and large shiny red fruit. Another species, black chokecherry (*Aronia melanocarpa*), is very similar to red chokecherry, but its fruit is a deep blackish purple. The fruit look like small blueberries but are not edible. This species is very useful in dry areas as well as wet, poorly drained areas of the garden.

{ *Callicarpa* spp.
Beautyberry

Beautyberry is a distinctive shrub with fall-fruiting interest that persists into the winter. Most of the year beautyberry will go unnoticed, but in late summer and early fall it begins to display clusters of small, pink flowers that develop into glossy, purple fruit. By late fall when the leaves shed, a brilliant display of fruit clusters are the highlight of the landscape. Although most shrubs appear to be done for the season, in the autumn beautyberry is just getting started.

Common beautyberry (*Callicarpa dichotoma*) is a medium-sized shrub with an upright and arching growth habit. This fast growing shrub will grow 4 ft. in height with a similar spread. During the summer, pink flower clusters line up along each stem and eventually develop into bunches of bright purple berries. In the Northeast, this shrub is at its best around Thanksgiving when the leaves have fallen to expose beautiful fruit. The fruit will typically remain on the plants until early winter, when the birds will devour them.

Beautyberry is suitable in small groupings, mass plantings, informal hedges, foundation plantings, or as a single specimen. The showy fruit are most handsome when highlighted by the winter sun. The varieties and species mentioned below are hardy from Zones 5–8 except for Bodinier beautyberry, which is hardy from Zones 6–8.

NOTABLE VARIETIES

'Albifructa'. This white-fruited form is very showy with milky white fruit that glow in the landscape.

Common beautyberry fruit lined up along the stem

Bodinier beautyberry in winter

'Early Amethyst'. An early-fruiting form producing a profusion of small, lilac-colored fruit.

'Issai'. This unique variety sets an abundance of fruit as a young plant, providing almost immediate satisfaction.

Bodinier beautyberry (*Callicarpa bodinieri* var. *giraldii* '*Profusion*'). Bodinier beautyberry has a strong, upright growth habit reaching 10 ft. in height. It is one of the best species for fruit display, yielding large, dark purple fruit. Leaf color ranges from yellow to purple in the fall.

Japanese beautyberry (*Callicarpa japonica*). Japanese beautyberry develops into a large, upright shrub and has violet purple fruit. 'Leucocarpa' is a white-fruited form that is usually showier than the purple-fruited form.

Cotoneaster spp.
Cotoneaster

Cotoneaster is a common flowering shrub that can be used in many different landscape situations. There are many species and varieties of cotoneaster, both deciduous and evergreen. Cotoneaster is quick to establish in the landscape and offers a graceful habit, delicate flowers, ornamental fruit, and brilliant fall foliage coloration.

Cotoneaster is susceptible to a variety of pests and diseases, but it will usually tolerate these problems if sited correctly. Pruning to remove dead or diseased branches can be done while the plant is dormant.

Cotoneasters thrive in full sun or partial shade and moist, well-drained soil, but will tolerate almost any landscape environment.

Cotoneaster is useful in groupings, mass plantings and foundation plantings. The low-growing species are effective along rock walls or the edges of garden beds.

Creeping cotoneaster (*Cotoneaster adpressus*)

This graceful, low-growing groundcover will eventually spread to 4–6 ft. The attractive, small, pink flowers provide a subtle display in spring and early summer. The delicate, dark green leaves also provide a fine texture in the garden. The foliage turns deep orange, red, and purple during the autumn, and these vibrant colors will persist for several weeks. One of the most attractive features of this ground-hugging plant is the cranberry red fruit that ripen in late summer and early fall. The fruit will remain after the leaves have fallen to provide winter interest. Hardy from Zones 4–7 but may need protection in Zone 4.

'Little Gem' is a charming, low-growing variety with dark, glossy green leaves and cascading sprays of branches. This compact plant is suitable along rock walls and is a good companion plant to low-growing perennials and dwarf conifers.

Rockspray cotoneaster (*Cotoneaster horizontalis*)

A low-growing cotoneaster, rockspray is very popular and has similar uses to creeping cotoneaster in the landscape. Rockspray cotoneaster offers a flowing, horizontally branched growth habit reaching 3 ft. in height and spreading 6–8 ft. wide. In addition to growing as a groundcover, it can also be trained up walls and fences like a vine. The petite foliage will also display shades of red, orange, and maroon in the autumn that are usually long lasting. The small, pink flowers are inconspicuous but develop into attractive bright red fruit in the fall. These fruit will persist into the winter. Collectively, the fruit display along with the elegant growth habit provides interest throughout the winter months.

Rockspray cotoneaster is best in full sun or partial shade where there is well-drained, moist soil. It is also very tolerant of drier soils. Pruning should be kept to a minimum so that the handsome growth habit is not disturbed. Selective pruning in late winter to remove old or dead branches is acceptable.

Rockspray cotoneaster is an excellent plant for fall and winter landscape effect. It is very useful in mass plantings, along rock walls, in raised planters, and as a companion plant to other dwarf shrubs. Hardy from Zones 5–7.

{ *Ilex* spp.
Deciduous hollies

Hollies are normally thought of as large evergreen forms that provide lush, dark green, spiny leaves and bright red fruit just in time for the holidays. Hollies are one of the most recognizable and widely used shrubs in the landscape. While they blend into the landscape most of the year, in winter they step to the forefront and are easily noticed in the bare winter landscape.

In addition to the evergreen types, there are several deciduous hollies species that drop their smooth, nonspiny leaves in the fall to show off their exquisite red berries. The fruit display of deciduous hollies is quite often even more impressive than its evergreen counterparts because the leaves do not hide the fruit. During the winter, the striking red fruit are the main attraction against the dark brown, naked stems.

Deciduous hollies present a great opportunity for gardeners who are craving a new look in the garden. Although evergreen hollies are quite popular and blanket many landscapes throughout the world, deciduous hollies are now emerging as highly cultivated, superior garden shrubs.

One very important and interesting feature that hollies possess is that they are dioecious. This means that while most plants have male and female flower parts on the same plant, male and female holly flowers are borne on separate plants. In order for female holly plants to bear fruit, a nearby male plant must pollinate them. 'Jim Dandy' is a male clone suitable to pollinate 'Autumn Glow', 'Harvest Red', and 'Red Sprite', while 'Southern Gentleman' is an excellent pollinator for 'Winter Red' and 'Sparkleberry'. One male plant will pollinate several female plants growing nearby.

Most of these species will develop into medium or large shrubs, although possum haw (*Ilex decidua*) can be trained as a small tree. Pruning should be kept to a minimum and only older, unproductive stems should be removed if necessary. Deciduous holly is ideal in groupings, mass plantings, or as a single specimen. When they reach a notable size in the landscape the branches can be harvested and used in holiday arrangements.

There are several species of deciduous hollies suitable for the home garden, a few of which are mentioned below.

Ilex verticillata (winterberry holly)
Winterberry holly is native from eastern Canada to the U.S.'s Midwest and Southeast. It freely grows in swampy areas along streams and low-lying areas in the woodland. But it is also a terrific landscape plant thriving in moist, well-drained garden soil.

Winterberry holly has glossy, bright red fruit that ripen in early fall and usually persist well into the winter months. These fruit glow against the backdrop of the winter landscape and are most evident in early winter when the fruit is fresh. The red berries are especially luminous after a freshly fallen snow. The berries are also a valuable source of food for birds, which relish them as a tasty treat. 'Harvest Red', 'Red Sprite', 'Winter Gold', and 'Winter Red' are all outstanding selections. Hardy from Zones 3–9.

Ilex serrata (Japanese winterberry)
Another notable species of deciduous holly is Japanese winterberry. A native of Japan and China, it is similar to *I. verticillata* except that the fruit are smaller. Several hybrids between this species and *I. verticillata* have yielded superb hybrid varieties, including 'Autumn Glow' and 'Sparkleberry'. Hardy from Zones 5–8.

Ilex decidua (possum haw)
Possum haw is another North American native that grows in woodlands and waterways of the southern

Winterberry holly berries

Winterberry holly in the landscape

United States and Mexico. It is a tall, upright shrub with smooth, glossy, green leaves during the summer that shed in autumn. Its red berries often persist through the winter. 'Warren's Red' is a good variety with deep, glossy, red berries. Hardy from Zones 5–9.

Malus spp.
Crabapple

There are about thirty species of crabapples growing in native habitats across Europe, Asia, and North America. In addition to numerous species, there are also hundreds of garden varieties of these highly cultivated trees. Although crabapples are best known

The profusion of fruit from 'Autumn Glow'

Ilex serrata 'Autumn Glow' in the landscape

The luscious fruit of Sugar Tyme crabapple in winter

for their beautiful white or pink flowers in spring, these popular flowering trees also offer interesting fruit and a picturesque growth habit with age. The dark brown, textured bark and artistic growth pattern of mature trees look spooky on cloudy, wintry days.

Crabapples have long been cultivated as ornamental trees for the home landscape. Their ability to adapt to many landscape situations and perform admirably sets them apart from many other flowering trees. Many of the older crabapple varieties are susceptible to various diseases that damage their leaves, stems, and fruit. These diseases include leaf spots, rust, apple scab, etc. However, over the past few years, extensive research has yielded superb varieties of crabapples that demonstrate improved disease resistance and superior ornamental characteristics.

While there are many excellent selections available today, two notable varieties are Sugar Tyme and Red Jewel. Both selections have glossy, bright red fruit that look like miniature candy apples clustered along each stem. These luscious fruit ripen in autumn and often persist through the winter. They are most beautiful on a clear winter's day when they sparkle under the bright sun. Other notable varieties include 'Callaway', 'Centurion', and *Malus* X *zumi* var. *calocarpa*.

Crabapples prefer moist, well-drained soil and full sun but are remarkably tolerant of wind, poor soils, pollution, shade, and temperature extremes. Pruning should be done in late spring or early summer after flowering. Crabapples can be used in small groupings or as a single specimen. Crabapples are useful in both residential and commercial landscape settings. Most crabapples are hardy from Zones 4–7.

{ *Rhus* spp.
Sumac

There are over 150 species of sumac, many of which are native to the United States. This diverse group of plants is a vital part of the natural woodland and seashore environment. Its most impressionable attributes are the spikes of red fruit and exquisite orange to fiery red fall foliage color.

Sumac is a very durable shrub or small tree that is especially suitable in barren, poor soils, and harsh, dry conditions. In a garden setting it will thrive and provide interest during the summer, autumn, and winter seasons. As the plant matures, sumac develops an irregular, picturesque growth habit that is rather handsome. All of these attributes make this plant a popular garden feature for all four seasons.

Rhus typhina (staghorn sumac)

Although there are several species of sumac that will perform well in the garden, staghorn sumac is the most popular and most commercially available. It has a large leaf consisting of many small leaflets that collectively extend one to two feet long. The bright green leaves change to brilliant shades of yellow, orange, and red in the fall and are sure to stop plant lovers in their tracks.

Staghorn sumac is dioecious, with male and female flowers borne on separate plants. In the summer, sumac will exhibit large, 4–8 in. long, cone-shaped greenish yellow flowers that transform into deep red fruit in the fall. The cone-shaped fruit spikes stand straight up and will

Staghorn sumac's distinctive red fruit

persist much of the winter. The fruit are an excellent source of high-protein food for migratory birds. The asymmetrical growth patterns of staghorn sumac become very beautiful with age. The thick stems are covered with velvety hairs and resemble a deer's antlers in the winter.

'Laciniata' is a female variety that has finely cut, fern-like leaves. It is a very delicate shrub that is useful in mass plantings, natural areas, and perennial borders.

This resilient native prefers full sun and moist, well-drained soil, but it will adapt to almost any landscape situation. It will thrive in hot, dry conditions and sandy soils. Although staghorn sumac will grow into a small tree, it can easily be maintained as a small- to medium-sized shrub with regular pruning. The plants can be selectively pruned in late winter to accomplish this goal.

Staghorn sumac is especially effective in seashore conditions, highly exposed areas, and hot, dry locations. It is also useful as a companion plant to smaller flowering shrubs and perennials. Hardy from Zones 4–8.

Viburnum spp.
Viburnum

Viburnum dilatatum (linden viburnum)

Linden viburnum is one of the most useful viburnums for small, residential landscapes. Linden viburnum has a dense growth habit and year-round interest. It displays showy white flowers, handsome foliage, and excellent fall-fruiting characteristics. In the summer season lustrous, dark green leaves provide an extraordinary texture before changing to deep red or maroon in the fall. The cranberry-like fruit are featured on the cover of this book.

White, flat-topped flowers emerge in mid spring and transform into clusters of bright red, cranberry-like fruit in autumn. The truly spectacular fruit display of linden viburnum will often last through the early part of the winter.

Linden viburnum is effective along the foundation of a house, in small groupings, mass plantings, and in woodland gardens. It grows best in Zones 5–7 but will grow in Zones 4 and 8 if sited in a protected area of the garden.

NOTABLE VARIETIES

'Asian Beauty'. The large, dark green leaves and bright red fruit are very handsome.

'Catskill'. Compact selection reaching 5–6 ft. in height.

'Erie'. A large-flowering selection with flowers up to 6 in. across. Excellent fruit-bearing variety.

'Michael Dodge'. An unusual selection with yellow fruit. It is a very nice accent plant to introduce something different into the garden.

Viburnum opulus and V. trilobum (cranberrybush viburnum)

The American and European cranberrybush viburnums are well-known garden favorites, displaying bright red, cranberry-like fruit from late summer through the fall. During the winter the fruit persist but usually wither as the cold temperatures become increasingly frigid.

Both species are very similar and are commercially available in the horticulture trade. Cranberrybush viburnums tend to set fruit more reliably when planted in groups where they will cross-pollinate. Cranberrybush viburnums offer white, flat-topped flowers in spring and a distinctive three-lobed leaf. Foliage will turn yellow, deep red, or maroon in the fall.

These dense, upright shrubs can grow to 12 ft. in height with a similar spread. For best flowering and fruit display, shrubs should be grown in full sun or partial shade. Cranberrybush viburnum prefers, moist, well-drained soil but is very adaptable to varying soil types.

Cranberrybush viburnum is an excellent choice for shade gardens, groupings, informal hedges, and screens. American cranberrybush is best suited to grow in Zones 2–7, while its European counterpart grows in Zones 3–8.

NOTABLE EUROPEAN CRANBERRYBUSH VARIETIES

'Compactum'. A compact variety only growing 6 ft. high and wide. It is an extremely dense plant with extraordinary fruit display in the fall. Excellent for the garden with limited space.

'Notcutt'. This variety offers large, white flowers, luscious, red fruit, and excellent maroon fall color. This selection is known as a reliable performer in the landscape.

NOTABLE AMERICAN CRANBERRYBUSH VARIETIES

'Compactum'. A compact, dense form with very attractive fruit. Like the compact variety of the European cranberrybush viburnum, this selection is very effective in residential landscapes.

Translucent fruit of American cranberrybush viburnum

'Wentworth'. Selected in the early 1900s for its larger, edible fruit. Fruit ripen gradually and change from yellow-red coloration to bright red.

Appreciating Our Big Trees

Our natural forests, public and private gardens, parks, and urban landscapes are graced with the beauty and strength of many species of deciduous trees. These trees provide shade, food, and shelter for the wildlife that depends so heavily on their existence. They also provide unfailing beauty and valuable landscape function to humans and improve our quality of life that will span generations. Although many of the trees listed below will grow too large for most residential landscapes, we must pay homage to their place in the landscape and appreciate them as nature's aristocrats. Our great trees are nature's living sculptures that tell the story of our past and provide hope for the future.

"Despite the gardener's
best intentions,
Nature will improvise."
—*Michael P. Garafalo*

{ *Fagus sylvatica* and *F. grandifolia* Beech

Beech trees are considered the noblest of deciduous trees. Their graceful, majestic growth habit and wide spreading branches are easily recognizable even from far away. Their smooth, silvery gray bark glistens in the winter landscape. Because of their size and stature, beeches have been used for centuries to create great landscapes for magnificent private estates, parks, arboretums, and other large sites throughout Europe and America.

Both of these species offer smooth bark that resembles an elephant's skin. On mature trees the bark often has patches of gnarled, irregular patterns that provide a nice contrast. American beech (*Fagus grandifolia*), a native to eastern North American forests, has a silvery gray bark that often appears nearly white. Native Americans referred to American beech as the "ghost tree" because of this characteristic. European beech (*Fagus sylvatica*), although similar in some respects to American beech, possesses a dull gray bark. The growth habit is rounded to oval, and the lower branches will sweep down toward the ground in a very graceful manner. Both species are exquisite in the winter, from their massive trunks to the smallest of branches. In addition to aesthetic value, European beech had agricultural value as well. During World Wars I and II, Europeans would collect the beechnut and extract oil to make a type of margarine.

Beech trees are large, hardwood relatives of oak and must be given adequate room to grow. Trees can easily reach 60–80 ft. high with similar width.

The smooth bark of European beech resembles elephant skin.

Gardeners enamored by these kings of the landscape should consider their presence long term. Beeches grow slowly, although they do grow reasonably fast

Beech in winter

when young. They can live for hundreds of years if properly maintained.

Beeches, like many other members of the oak family, thrive in moist, organic, and well-drained loamy soil. In addition, it is imperative that beech specimens are provided with mulch, compost, or similar organic materials (1–2 in. thick) on the surface of the soil. This encourages naturally occurring soilborne organisms known as mycorrhizae that live in the soil to help the tree absorb water and nutrients.

One of the most impressive characteristics of beech is the pronounced trunk flare or buttress that forms on older trees. This flare is located at the base of the tree and can be quite artistic on older trees. Beech does best in full sun but will also tolerate partial shade. As beech matures it will eventually cast deep shade as it grows into a large specimen.

European beech is widespread throughout Europe and is found both in the natural forest and cultivated landscapes throughout the countryside. It has adapted

> "I frequently tramped eight or ten miles through the deepest snow to keep an appointment with a beech-tree, or a yellow birch, or an old acquaintance among the pines."
> — *Henry David Thoreau*

to North American climates and was heavily used during the late nineteenth and early twentieth centuries. European beech is a highly cultivated tree with dozens of garden varieties to choose from. These garden varieties offer weeping and columnar habits and a variety of summer foliage colors (purple, gold, variegated, etc.). Although American beech is primarily found in the natural woodland, it can also be grown as a shade tree in a large, open lawn area. Beeches are hardy from Zones 4–7.

Structure of sycamore in winter

{ *Platanus occidentalis* American sycamore

American sycamore is a very important North American native tree. In the landscape, American sycamore is found along streets, urban sites, parks, and in other open areas. This particular species is best admired in the natural forest environment or a large park and should not necessarily be planted in the residential landscape because of its ultimate size.

American sycamore can reach 70 ft. or taller and is just too big and messy for the average home garden.

In a natural setting, this strong, sturdy tree has beautiful exfoliating bark that sheds in large sheets, exposing a multicolored underbark of cream, green, and brown. This smooth multicolored bark makes this tree one of the most identifiable.

American sycamore is a tough, adaptable shade tree, tolerating variable landscape conditions such as poor soils, windy conditions, soil compaction, and drought. American sycamore is hardy from Zones 4–9.

Exfoliating bark of sycamore

While sycamore is a resilient tree, it is susceptible to a host of damaging diseases, including anthracnose, which is a serious leaf disease that can defoliate the tree during cool, moist spring weather. London planetree (*Platanus* × *acerifolia*) is a hybrid that is similar in many respects to sycamore but is more tolerant of pests and urban conditions. London planetree should also be sited in large, open areas. There are several select varieties that have shown good resistance to disease,

including 'Bloodgood', 'Columbia', 'Liberty', and 'Yarwood'.

Quercus spp.
The mighty oak

To many, the oak tree is considered the king of the forest. It has been an important part of culture and religion since ancient times. The Greeks, Romans, and Druids all worshiped the oak, and in many cultures it came to symbolize protection, strength, stability, and comfort. Recently the oak tree became the national tree of the United States.

There are about 450 species of oak growing all over the world. In general, oaks are slow-growing, hardwood trees that offer grace and beauty in natural and cultivated landscapes across the globe. Oaks are long-lived trees that can survive for hundreds of years. They provide cool shade in the summer and a rich assortment of brilliant orange, red, or rusty brown fall foliage colors. During the winter months, their bare, dark silhouettes make a visual impact from any part of the garden.

Oaks furnish shelter and habitat for wildlife, and their acorns (nuts) provide a very important source of high protein food for animals. In the garden, oaks are like faithful friends, rarely disappointing and always making their presence known. In the winter landscape, oak trees are strong, stately fixtures, providing strength and structure to the garden. Regardless of harsh weather and the ever-changing world around them, oaks always seem to endure.

Oaks prefer moist, well-drained, acidic soil that is rich in leaf litter and other forms of organic matter.

Vincent A. Simeone

The mighty red oak in winter

White oak in a snowy winter landscape

Oaks thrive in full sun or partial shade and are extremely adaptable to a wide range of environmental conditions.

While there are many oaks that are worthy of introduction into expansive landscapes, here are a few species commonly found in nature that are also great additions to the landscape with room to accommodate them. Oaks are generally hardy from Zones 3–9, but the exact hardiness depends on the individual species.

- White oak (*Quercus alba*)
- Scarlet oak (*Quercus coccinea*)
- Burr oak (*Quercus macrocarpa*)
- Water oak (*Quercus nigra*)
- Pin oak (*Quercus palustris*)
- Red oak (*Quercus rubra*)
- Black oak (*Quercus velutina*)

"The monarch oak,
the patriarch of the trees,
Shoots rising up,
and spreads by slow degrees.
Three centuries he grows,
and three he stays
Supreme in state;
and in three more decays."
—*John Dryden*

Whether they are young seedlings to be planted or well-developed young trees purchased at a local nursery, oak trees should be consider sacred additions to any landscape. They act as guardians of the landscape and link us to our past while offering hope for our future generations.

Ulmus spp.
Elm

Elms are fast-growing, durable landscape trees that provide shade in the summer and structure in the winter. They are very adaptable, tolerating poor soils, pollution, heat, drought, and other harsh conditions. In addition to their hardy nature, elms are also very beautiful specimen trees that have a wide variety of landscape uses.

Ulmus americana (American elm)

American elm has long been regarded as one of the most stately of the large shade trees. The tall, central trunk and cascading side branches give this tree a vase-shaped appearance. The bark is light brown or gray and develops a course texture as it matures. The lush, large, green leaves turn brilliant shades of golden yellow in the fall. These picturesque specimens are equally beautiful during the winter season, their branches swaying in the wind of a cold winter's day.

For decades, thousands of American elms lined the streets in many neighborhoods across America. But a devastating disease known as Dutch elm disease (DED) killed enormous amounts of these established trees. However, through important research, several new and improved cultivated varieties have been developed and show promising resistance to DED. 'Princeton' is a vigorous, fast-growing form with large, leathery leaves that is being touted for its DED resistance. 'Valley Forge' has a classic vase-shaped habit, dense canopy, and also shows excellent resistant to DED. American elm can grow 60–80 ft. tall and must be sited specifically where it has plenty of room. It can be used as a single specimen as a shade tree or in groupings. It was widely used as a street tree and can still be found en masse along city streets in Washington, D.C. Hardy from Zones 3–9.

Ulmus parviflora (Chinese elm)

Although Chinese elm does not typically get to the size and stature of American elm, it can still grow 30–50 ft. tall. The small, glossy, dark green leaves are

Vincent A. Simeone

Beautiful vase shape of American elm

Vincent A. Simeone

Orange-brown exfoliating bark of Allee elm

much finer than those of American elm. The leaves will turn yellow, deep red, or maroon in the fall. Chinese elm also displays a handsome, flaking bark with rich tones of orange, brown, gray, green, and tan. The bark interest is truly spectacular during the winter season. Two excellent varieties growing on the campus of the University of Georgia have been select-

ed and introduced. Allee ('Emerald Vase') is a tall variety with a vase-shaped habit, dark green foliage, and showy reddish orange exfoliating bark. Athena ('Emerald Isle') has a mounded canopy with exceptionally dark green foliage and beautiful exfoliating bark. Hardy from Zones 4–9.

Evergreens

PART 2

An evergreen is defined as a plant that retains its leaves throughout the year. Evergreens add distinct beauty and structure to the landscape. In general terms, evergreens are classified as either broadleaf or narrow leaved. Narrow-leaved evergreens—also referred to as needled evergreens, such as pines and spruce—have thin, needle-like foliage. Evergreen plants, such as holly and rhododendron, that have wide leaves are known as broadleaf evergreens.

Broadleaf Evergreens

The term "evergreen" is relative given the fact that all evergreens eventually lose their older leaves. Most evergreens retain their foliage for several years, but new foliage eventually replaces the older. For example, during the fall, the older foliage/leaves of holly trees will drop, littering the ground, while the newest growth is retained.

The following evergreens are excellent additions to the winter landscape. They provide rich foliage color and pleasing textures that present a beautiful backdrop or a focal point in the landscape. In addition to superior foliage, many of the broadleaf evergreens also display beautiful flowers and fruit. Whether used as a single specimen or in groupings, evergreens are an integral part of the garden and are most apparent during the winter season.

> "How important is the evergreen to the winter, that portion of the summer which does not fade."
> —*Henry David Thoreau*

Gold dust plant with its notable speckled foliage

Bright yellow leaves of *Aucuba*

Aucuba japonica 'Variegata'
Gold dust plant

This stunning shrub is a fine example of the beauty that broadleaf evergreens can add to the landscape. This cultivated variety—as well as 'Picturata' and 'Sulphur'—offers dark, lustrous, green leaves with speckles, splashes, and blotches of gold or yellow that look like patterns on a painter's canvas. Gold dust plant also has thick, smooth, green stems. Healthy plants can reach 6–10 ft. high with slightly less spread.

Aucuba prefers partial shade and well-drained, moist soil with ample amounts of organic matter. It will tolerate dense shade but beware of placing it in full sun, which will result in bleaching or scalding of the leaves. Pruning can be kept to a minimum but occasional selective pruning to remove old, weak stems is advisable. Stems can also be harvested and used for decorations during the holidays.

Gold dust plant makes a bold statement in the landscape and is suitable in groupings, mass plantings, shade gardens, and as a companion plant to rhododendrons and azaleas. This ornamental shrub is typically grown for its foliage and is very effective as an accent plant to brighten up a shady area of the garden. Hardy from Zones 7–10 but will grow in Zone 6 in a protected location.

{ *Berberis julianae*
Wintergreen barberry

This stout, mounded evergreen has glossy green leaves that change to bronzy red during the cold winter months. Wintergreen barberry is a robust grower that forms a dense, rounded mass of growth reaching 6–8 ft. or more in height. In early spring, bright golden yellow flowers form in clusters along each stem.

Wintergreen barberry is an extremely tough shrub, tolerating most soil types provided they are in a well-drained location. For best results, this evergreen barberry should be planted in moist, acidic, well-drained soil. It is remarkably tolerant of heat, drought, cold, and sandy or heavy clay soils. It will also tolerate shade but performs best in full sun.

Since barberry has sharp thorns extending several inches, careful siting should be considered when planting this shrub. Wintergreen barberry is effective in mass plantings or groupings, as an informal hedge or as a barrier planting. Hardy from Zones 5–8.

{ *Camellia* spp.
Camellia

Camellias have an extensive, rich garden history and have long been admired as one of the most exotic and showy evergreen flowering shrubs. In the eighteenth century, camellias were imported to Europe and America from Japan and China, where they grow in the higher elevations of the mountains. For many years they were thought to be tender and only considered for greenhouse collections especially in colder climates. But in several parts of the United

Camellia flowers and foliage

States, such as the Southeast and West Coast, camellias will grow outdoors. There are two main species valued as garden ornamentals in America: Japanese camellia (*Camellia japonica*) and sasanqua camellia (*Camellia sasanqua*). These ornamental camellias are close relatives to the tea plant (*Camellia sinensis*), a major economic crop that is used to manufacture tea.

Camellia flowers are incredibly diverse, with many different flower colors and types to choose from. Flower colors range from white to pink to red and even display two colors on the same flower. Camellia flower types can also vary from single to semi-double or double and can mimic other flowers such as peonies and anemones. Equally striking is camellia foliage, which is a handsome, glossy, dark green.

Hardy camellia in the landscape

Camellias have specific cultural needs similar to rhododendrons. They thrive in moist, well-drained, acidic soil with high organic content. Camellias also prefer light shade and mulch, which will help to protect their shallow root system. Several pests, including scale and spider mites, bother camellias. If a pest problem occurs, take a sample to your local agricultural extension service for evaluation and suggested treatment.

Pruning to shape plants or maintain dense habits can be done after flowering. If severe pruning is needed, wait until late winter or early spring, when shrubs are dormant. This type of pruning will reduce flowering the first year but will stimulate the plant to produce a healthy crop of flowers the next few years after that. In general, regular, excessive pruning should be avoided. Camellias can reach 8–12 ft. in height and 6–10 ft. wide but can be kept smaller with judicious pruning. Although camellias thrive in moist, cool environments, they are remarkably tolerant of hot, humid conditions, provided they are watered properly.

Camellias are excellent flowering shrubs to add structure and beauty to the home landscape. The colorful flowers, strong growth habit, and lustrous foliage offer great texture and vibrant colors in the garden. Camellias can be used in groupings and shade gardens and can also be utilized as informal hedges, screens, or as individual specimens.

While camellias have traditionally been considered landscape favorites for warmer, moderated climates, extensive research has produced many new, cold-hardy varieties that can be used in northern climates. The majority of these cold hardy selections are the result of extensive work done by two scientists, Dr. Ackerman and Dr. Parks. The Ackerman hybrids are primarily hybrids of several different species, while the Parks selections are hybrids and choice Japanese camellia varieties. These resilient shrubs flower in either fall or spring, depending on the species and variety chosen. The Japanese camellia varieties normally flower from early to late spring, and the *C. sasanqua* hybrids bloom in late fall. In either case, camellias used in colder climates outdoors should be sited carefully and protected from cold, windy, and exposed areas of the garden.

One key element in successfully growing camellias is the time of year they are planted. To ensure your camellia plants establish quickly, they should be planted at a time when weather conditions are mild and optimum for root growth. For example, in the north, camellias should be planted in spring, after the harsh, cold winter temperatures have subsided. Plants will develop root and top growth during the spring and summer before the onset of the cooler temperatures of autumn. In addition, camellias planted in these colder climates should be given northern or western exposure to avoid morning sun in winter. To further protect your camellias, individual plants can be wrapped with burlap or sprayed with anti-dessicants. If sited incorrectly, camellias are more susceptible to winter damage and leaf desiccation. The contrary is true of gardens in the south, where fall planting is recommended after the harsh heat of the summer has passed. In this situation, camellias planted in the fall in southern gardens will establish roots during the cooler season before the scorching heat of summer approaches.

Although there are many fine hardy camellia selections available, here are a few garden-worthy varieties to begin your journey with this fine garden plant. The selections discussed below are most reliable in Zones 7–9, although they will also grow in Zone 6 if properly sited.

Camellia japonica (Japanese camellia)
NOTABLE VARIETIES

'April Blush'. This variety grows into a bushy plant with deep green leaves and shell pink, semi-double blooms.

'April Rose'. This compact and rather slow-growing plant has rose red, double flowers. It is very floriferous

Bicolored camellia bloom

and will bloom in mid spring.

'April Snow'. This relatively slow-growing plant has white, rose-form double flowers. It provides a profuse display of color in mid to late spring.

'Kumasaka'. One of the oldest varieties of camellia, this has been grown in Japan since 1695. The double blooms are red or deep rose and open late in spring.

'Lady Clare'. This variety has semi-double pink flowers.

Camellia hybrids

NOTABLE VARIETIES

'Pink Icicle'. This hybrid from Dr. Ackerman has shell pink, peony-like flowers in early spring. The dark green leaves tolerate winter sun and make a nice background for the large flowers.

'Polar Ice'. The white double flowers open in mid fall on upright branches. The plant will grow to 6 ft. by 6 ft. in ten years.

'Winter's Rose'. This dwarf camellia grows 3 ft. wide and 3–4 ft. tall. The pale pink double flowers are produced in profusion in mid to late fall.

'Winter's Star'. Single flowers are a reddish purple and emerge in mid to late fall.

Sasanqua camellia (*Camellia sasanqua*)

In addition to Japanese camellia and their hybrids, sasanqua camellia can really brighten up the autumn and early winter with their wonderful white, pink, or red flowers. This species is generally smaller than Japanese camellia, growing 6–10 ft. tall. The plant also has a finer texture than Japanese camellia, with deli-

Single camellia bloom

'Winter's Star' flower

cate flowers and petite glossy leaves. It is hardy from Zones 7–9 but should be protected in northern gardens. 'Cleopatra' is a very strong grower with pink, semi-double flowers and an upright habit.

Cotoneaster salicifolius
Willow cotoneaster

Willow cotoneaster has a graceful, weeping growth habit and long, slender, dark evergreen leaves. The bright reddish orange fruit will ripen in the fall and persist through the winter. Mature shrubs can reach 10–15 ft. high with handsome, arching branches.

Willow cotoneaster performs best in well-drained, acidic soil and full sun or partial shade. Regular selective pruning to remove older branches will encourage dense, healthy growth. Willow cotoneaster is useful as a specimen plant near the foundation of a house or in small groupings. 'Scarlet Leader' is a low-growing form that can be used in a mass planting. Hardy in Zones 6–7.

Daphne odora
Winter daphne

This beautiful evergreen has delicate purple flower buds that open to pinkish white flowers in mid to late winter. The flowers give off a sweet fragrance that will quickly catch the attention of a passing visitor to the garden. The dark, glossy, green leaves offer a rich, bold texture in the landscape. This dense shrub is a reliable performer in warmer climates and can also be grown in containers and brought indoors in northern climates. Winter daphne will grow 3–4 ft. or more tall with an equal spread.

Winter daphne is an adaptable shrub that will thrive in moist, well-drained soil and partial shade. This winter-blooming shrub can effectively be used in groupings, woodland gardens, foundation plantings, and is especially useful in containers. Bringing the plant into a sunroom during the winter will provide weeks of wonderful fragrance. Apparently all parts of the plant are highly toxic if eaten, so keep it away from children and pets. Hardy from Zones 7–9.

'Aureomarginata' is a striking variegated form with yellow leaf edges. Hardier than the species, it will survive the northern limits of Zone 7 and possibly Zone 6 with protection.

Ilex spp.
Holly

There are few broadleaf evergreens that can provide the visual impact or achieve the grand stature of a specimen holly tree. While they blend into the landscape most of the year, in late autumn as the berries ripen, these picturesque evergreens seem to come to life with landscape interest. Evergreen hollies are grown for their beautiful foliage, showy fruit, and dense growth habit. In general, hollies are easy-to-grow, adaptable landscape plants that tolerate pruning and varying soil types, soil pH, and light exposures.

One very important fact about hollies is that they are dioecious, meaning male and female flowers are borne on separate plants. Therefore, female plants need male pollinators in order to bear fruit. One male plant nearby can pollinate many female plants; however, like species should be used in pollination. For example, an

John Bieber

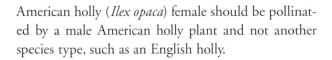

Foliage and flower of *Daphne odora* 'Aureomarginata'

English holly berries

American holly (*Ilex opaca*) female should be pollinated by a male American holly plant and not another species type, such as an English holly.

Ilex aquifolium (English holly)

English holly has beautiful, glossy foliage that glistens in the sun during the winter. The leaves have a lustrous finish that reflects the sunlight. The species name, *aquifolium*, refers to the spiny leaves, so you need to handle this plant with care. During the fall, large, juicy, red fruit ripen and typically last most of the winter until birds pick them off the stems. The tall, pyramidal growth habit and horizontal side branches provide a firm figure in the landscape. There are many cultivated varieties of English holly available, with selections offering red or yellow berries, variegated foliage, and various growth patterns.

English holly prefers moist, well-drained, acidic soil and full sun or partial shade. It does not do particularly well in windy, exposed sites and can suffer from leaf burn during the winter. This is caused by a combination of cold temperatures and strong, drying winds. In most cases the damaged leaves will fall in the spring and will be replaced with new leaves. This species can grow over 20 ft. tall, so adequate room is needed to accommodate its robust size.

English holly can be grown as a single specimen, in groupings, as a screening plant, or as a hedge. The cut branches are highly valued during the holiday season and are used in arrangements and holiday displays. Hardy from Zones 6–7.

Ilex glabra (inkberry holly)

This hardy native is found in natural habitats from

eastern Canada to the southeastern and midwestern United States Inkberry holly has a much different appearance than most traditional holly species. It has smooth, lush, dark green leaves with no spines. It bears a small, black fruit in the fall that will persist most of the winter.

Inkberry holly is an extremely adaptable plant that is able to grow in a variety of landscape situations, from a shady woodland to a hot, dry sunny location near the seashore. In the garden, inkberry holly performs best in acidic, well-drained, loamy soil and full sun or partial shade.

Inkberry holly can be used effectively as a hedge, screen, mass planting, or foundation planting. Well-established plants can reach 6–8 ft. tall and wide.

There are numerous varieties that are pleasant additions to the garden, including 'Compacta', 'Nigra', and 'Shamrock'. 'Compacta' is a slower-growing variety that will not grow as large as the species and it is more suitable for smaller garden settings. Hardy from Zones 4–10 but should be protected in 4 and 10.

Ilex x meserveae (blue holly)

Mrs. F. Leighton Meserve of Long Island, New York, produced the Meserve hybrid hollies in the early 1950s. To create these wonderful hybrid hollies, Mrs. Meserve hybridized the prostrate holly (*Ilex rugosa*), known for its cold tolerance and shrubby habit, and the English Holly (*Ilex aquifolium*), possessing luxurious, glossy foliage. Since the 1960s, many garden varieties have emerged, including 'Blue Boy', 'Blue Girl', Blue Prince, Blue Princess, China Girl, and Dragon Lady.

Blue hollies have small, dark green leaves and deep purple stems. The leaves have a distinct leathery texture. Many of the blue holly varieties grow 8 ft. or more wide and high, developing into a thick mass of stems and leaves. Dragon Lady is the exception, with an upright, pyramidal habit to 15 ft. high. Blue hollies have bright red fruit that are rather attractive against the dark canvas of the foliage.

Blue hollies are excellent landscape plants suitable for home gardens in the northern and midwestern United States. They are best suited in Zones 5–7 but will tolerate certain parts of Zone 4 as well if sited and in a protected location. These hybrids do not perform particularly well in warmer climates that have excessive heat and humidity. Because of their shrubby habit, blue hollies can be used as screening plants, hedges, and in a foundation planting.

Ilex opaca (American holly)

American holly, like English holly, will grow tall and should be sited where it has plenty of room in the garden. American holly has dull or semi-glossy green, spiny, leaves and a dense, pyramidal growth habit with strong, lateral branches. The red berries also have a dull sheen but are quite conspicuous clustered along each stem. 'Canary' is a yellow-fruited form that will complement the red-fruited varieties very well. As American holly matures, it develops smooth, light brown or gray bark with rough textured accents.

American holly is very durable in the landscape and can tolerate a variety of soil types, light exposures, wind, salt spray, and heat. Ideally, American holly should receive moist, well-drained, acidic soil and full sun or partial shade.

American holly can offer a bold statement in the winter landscape with its tall, dense growth habit and broad, thick leaves. It is versatile and can be used as a specimen, formal or informal hedge, screen, or is adaptable as a woodland plant. Hardy from Zones 5–9.

Ilex pedunculosa (longstalk holly)

This unusual Asian species has somewhat of a tropical look in the garden; the foliage resembles the tropical *Ficus benjamina*, the popular houseplant. The smooth, wavy, green leaves have no spines, and the dense, upright growth habit stands out in the landscape. This species can be trained into a tree reaching 20 ft. or

Yellow-fruited American holly 'Canary'

American holly in winter

more in height. Longstalk holly produces deep red fruit attached to the branches by long stems.

This cold-hardy species is ideal in northern climates and performs best in Zones 5–7. Longstalk holly is equally effective as a single specimen or in groupings. It is truly an exceptional evergreen for the plant collector with a keen eye for the unusual.

Kalmia latifolia
Mountain laurel

Mountain laurel is an exquisite native shrub growing from eastern Canada to the southern States. In addition to its presence in the natural woodland, mountain laurel is a very valuable ornamental for the home land-scape. Extensive breeding since the 1960s has produced many exceptional garden varieties with dense growth habit and blooms available in a variety of colors.

Although mountain laurel is a relatively slow grower, it offers numerous ornamental qualities to the patient gardener. In spring, rounded clusters of white, pink, or rose-colored flowers sit atop the dark green leaves. The individual flower buds are star shaped and collectively create a spectacular floral display as they open. Some of the more recent varieties offer a striking, two-tone, banded coloration. Older specimens reveal a beautifully textured, brown bark and irregular growth habit that are most noticeable in winter.

Smooth foliage and berries of longstalk holly

Mountain laurel's textured bark

Mountain laurels prefer moist, well-drained, acidic soil and full sun or partial shade. They are quite adaptable and will tolerate a variety of soils, light exposures, and even drought. Overgrown or poorly shaped shrubs can be easily rejuvenated by severely pruning the plant in early spring down to about 12 in. In spring, new growth will develop from hidden growth buds that are present along the stems. This type of pruning will create a compact, vigorous plant.

Mountain laurel is an ideal woodland shrub and is also effective in small groupings, foundation plantings, and as a screening plant. Small, dwarf garden varieties such as 'Elf', 'Little Linda', and 'Minuet' are effective in combination with other dwarf plants, such as low-growing perennials. Hardy from Zones 4–9.

NOTABLE VARIETIES

There are many new cultivated varieties of mountain laurel available for the home garden. These new varieties are compact and offer many flower colors. The varieties listed below are a modest representation of available selections.

'Carousel'. Flowers display a conspicuous purple banding.

'Elf'. A compact grower with light pink buds that open to pure white flowers.

'Minuet'. A dwarf growth habit with thin, glossy leaves. The pink buds open to creamy white flowers with deep maroon bands.

'Olympic Fire'. The red buds open to vivid pink flowers.

'Raspberry Glow'. Deep red buds open to raspberry pink flowers.

'Sarah'. This variety has striking red flower buds that open to reveal deep pink flowers.

{ *Leucothoe fontanesiana*
Drooping leucothoe

Drooping leucothoe is a common evergreen shrub that offers dark, glossy green foliage and a graceful growth habit. The smooth, pointed leaves are neatly arranged along drooping stems, providing a cascading effect. This native shrub will grow 3–6 ft. wide and several feet high. In spring, delicate white, fragrant, urn-shaped flowers hang from the base of the leaves. Upon the arrival of colder temperatures in winter, the leaves turn burgundy purple.

Drooping leucothoe thrives in moist, acidic, organic, well-drained soils. Partial shade is best, but it will also tolerate dense shade. Leucothoe may be grown in full sun provided it can be protected from high winds and adequate moisture can be supplied. This plant does best if sited in the coolest, shadiest part of the garden. Selective or renewal pruning should be done in early spring.

Leucothoe is very effective in woodland gardens and can also be used in mass plantings with rhododendrons and azaleas. Hardy from Zones 5–8 and Zone 4 with protection.

NOTABLE VARIETIES

'Girard's Rainbow'. This variety has interesting combinations of green, white, and pink in the leaf. It is a nice accent plant to add interest to an area of the garden that needs a splash of color.

'Scarletta'. The new growth is emerges glossy scarlet red and matures to deep green. The leaves turn brilliant burgundy red in winter.

{ *Magnolia grandiflora*
Southern magnolia

Southern magnolia is native to the southeastern United States. It is among the most beautiful broadleaf evergreens in the winter landscape, prominently displaying lush, coarse foliage and an upright, dense growth habit. Although it has long been a popular favorite in southern gardens, several new varieties of this plant will also grow and can be found in colder areas of the States, including Zone 6.

Southern magnolia has large, shiny, dark green leaves that can reach 6 in. or more in length. Certain specimens or select varieties display a rusty brown coloration to the underside of the leaves, which adds a nice contrast in the landscape. The broad, upright, and typically pyramidal growth habit has a distinct presence in the winter landscape. Southern magnolia will flower later than most deciduous types of magnolia with large, fragrant, white flowers emerging in summer. The spectacular flowers are followed by large, conelike fruit that ripen in the autumn and often persist through the winter. These interesting fruit are comprised of many small capsules, which will open to expose bright red seeds.

Southern magnolia is a remarkably resilient tree, preferring moist, well-drained, acidic soils and full sun or partial shade. It will tolerate poor soils including heavy clay and sandy loam soils. In northern climates,

Southern magnolia foliage

Vincent A. Simeone

southern magnolia can be planted in full sun or partial shade but should be sheltered from wind.

Southern magnolia can develop into a large tree, especially in warmer climates, and it must be given ample room to grow. Mature specimens can grow 60 ft. high or more in the South, although trees remain much smaller in colder climates. Southern magnolia can be used as a single specimen or in groupings. It is also a shade-tolerant tree and can be effectively used as a screening plant. However it is used, southern magnolia is sure to make a visual impact in the landscape. Hardy from Zones 6–9, but the best specimens can be found in the southern states.

'Edith Bogue' is one of the most popular and cold-hardy varieties of southern magnolia. 'Brackens Brown

Fuzzy buds of saucer magnolia in winter

Beauty' is an excellent selection with deep green, glossy foliage above and a rusty brown texture on the underside of the foliage. 'Little Gem' is a dwarf variety reaching up to 20 ft. high.

Although the evergreen magnolias are obvious choices for the winter landscape, the deciduous magnolias also add winter interest since they display soft, fuzzy flower buds while dormant. In spring, these fuzzy buds burst open to reveal beautiful white, pink, and deep purple flowers, depending on the species. The smooth, gray magnolia bark is also very noticeable in winter. Saucer magnolia (*Magnolia* × *soulangiana*), star magnolia (*Magnolia stellata*), and their hybrids are just a few examples of these interesting deciduous flowering trees.

{ *Mahonia* spp.
Mahonia

Mahonia is a close relative of barberry and one of the most peculiar looking evergreens in the landscape. These shrubby mahonia exhibit an upright, umbrella-like growth habit and thick, leathery leaves that are noticeable from afar.

While there are many species of *Mahonia,* the two Asian species presented in this section are worthwhile garden inhabitants. Leatherleaf mahonia (*Mahonia bealei*) has coarse, leathery, glossy leaves that appear artificial at first glance. The leaves are comprised of many small, spiny leaflets that collectively make up the entire leaf. Leaves can reach well over a foot long. Plants can grow 6–10 ft. high, displaying an open, irregular growth pattern over time. In late winter and early spring, clusters of fragrant, yellow flowers open and persist for several weeks. The flowers and glossy foliage are a rather handsome combination. After the flowers fade, small, deep blue, egg-shaped fruit form and will provide a tasty treat for birds.

Another mahonia that has garden merit is the Japanese mahonia (*Mahonia japonica*). Japanese mahonia is similar in all respects to leatherleaf mahonia but its individual flowers are brighter yellow and slightly larger.

Both species are very adaptable in the landscape and tolerate a range of soils and light exposures. Mahonia is extremely shade tolerant and will grow even in low-light situations. For best results, mahonia should be grown in well-drained, acidic soils and partial shade. Mahonia is very effective in small group-

Leatherleaf mahonia

ings or as a single specimen in a shady part of the garden. Mahonia adds interesting, bold texture and will shine in the winter landscape. Hardy from Zones 6–8.

A hybrid mahonia (*Mahonia* x *media*) is also gaining in popularity. It is often found growing in English gardens but is becoming more prevalent in American gardens. This hybrid displays rich, golden yellow flowers in late fall or early winter. It does perform best in the milder climates of the southeastern or northwestern United States. Hardy from Zones 7–9, but it will tolerate Zone 6 if planted in a protected location. 'Charity' and 'Winter Sun' are two excellent selections.

{ *Nandina domestica*
Heavenly bamboo

Although the common name for this shrub is heavenly bamboo, it is not related to the aggressive bamboo plants known throughout the world. Heavenly bamboo is a native of China and forms a rather neat clump of long, thin stems that will reach 6–8 ft. tall. The clumps of growth will spread by underground stems, but it is not typically invasive in the landscape.

The dark green, shiny leaves are made up of many small leaflets that collectively offer a fine, lacy appearance. The foliage will form dense, flat-topped clusters at the end of each branch and turn beautiful shades of reddish green in winter. In spring, the small, white flowers form at the ends of the stems. In the autumn, bright red fruit clusters ripen and will persist through the winter. The fruit display can be quite dramatic, and fruit are very useful for holiday decorating.

Heavenly bamboo does need regular pruning to remove old, thick stems. Careful selective removal of these stems will produce a healthier, vigorous, and densely growing plant. Unpruned shrubs will become tall and leggy and will lose their dense habit over time. Pruning should be performed in late winter or early spring, while shrubs are still dormant.

Heavenly bamboo is a delightful multistemmed shrub that is remarkably durable in the landscape. It will grow in a variety of soils and light exposures and is especially tolerant of dense shade. For best results, heavenly bamboo should be planted in groupings in full sun or partial shade and in moist, well-drained soil. Heavenly bamboo is also a great companion plant

Bright red fruit of heavenly bamboo

Winter color of 'Woods Dwarf' heavenly bamboo

to other broadleaf evergreens and shade-loving plants such as rhododendrons, hollies, and mahonia. There are many cultivated varieties of this shrub, and even a modest amount of research by the curious gardener will uncover numerous selections offering various foliage colors and growth habits. Two choice low-growing forms, 'Harbour Dwarf' and 'Woods Dwarf', are useful in gardens with limited space and are ideal as companion plants to other dwarf shrubs and perennials. Both dwarf varieties grow 2–3 ft. tall and have lacy, chartreuse green foliage with a tinge of reddish purple during the summer. In the winter, 'Harbour Dwarf' foliage turns reddish purple and 'Woods Dwarf' foliage turns a bright, crimson red. Both are excellent for winter foliage and will accent the winter garden.

Hardy from Zones 6–9.

Osmanthus heterophyllus
Holly osmanthus

Holly osmanthus, also known as false holly, is a tall, spreading shrub that has spiny, holly-like foliage but is actually related to lilac and forsythia. The dark, rich green foliage has a smooth texture with spiny edges. Small, inconspicuous flowers open in the autumn and may persist into early winter. The fragrance of the flowers can be quite potent.

Holly osmanthus has a shrubby growth habit when young but can become tall with a rounded habit as it matures. Individual plants can grow 8–15 ft. tall. These tall shrubs prefer well-drained, acidic soil and full sun or partial shade, but this species is also very tolerant of poor soils, drought, and low-light situations.

Holly osmanthus is very tolerant of pruning and can be grown as a formal or informal hedge. It is also effective as a screen or single specimen. 'Goshiki' is a peculiar looking variety with a swirled variegated pattern on the surface of the foliage. This selection is very effective as an accent in a partially shaded area of the garden. Hardy from Zones 6–9.

{ *Pieris japonica*
{ Pieris

Like rhododendron and mountain laurel, Japanese pieris is a very popular flowering shrub for the home landscape. The small, hanging flower buds are obvious in winter and develop into dangling white bell-like flowers in early spring. The fragrant flower clusters will last for several weeks or longer if the weather conditions are mild. In addition to the white flowering varieties, there are several pink flowering varieties that form clusters of noticeable pink or red flower buds in winter before opening in spring. The dark, glossy green leaves provide the perfect canvas to the showy blooms. As plants mature, they develop thick stems and rough fissured brown bark, which is very attractive in winter. Japanese pieris can grow up to 12 ft. high, but in most residential landscape situations can be maintained at 6–8 ft. tall.

This popular evergreen performs best in moist, well-drained, acidic soil and partial shade. This shrub will not perform well in full sun or highly exposed sites. Japanese pieris can be selectively pruned to maintain a

Pieris in the landscape

Clusters of pieris flower buds

dense habit. Poorly shaped plants can also be rejuvenated by severely pruning plants to 12 in. in early spring; however, the shrubs must be in good health.

Japanese pieris is effective in mass plantings, groupings, foundation plantings, woodland gardens, and as a screening plant. Hardy from Zones 5–7 and will grow in Zone 4 with protection.

NOTABLE VARIETIES

'Cavatine'. A later-blooming, dwarf form that is exceptionally cold hardy.

'Dorothy Wycoff'. Striking, dark red flower buds open to pale pink flowers.

'Valley Valentine'. This variety offers dark green foliage and rich maroon flower buds that open to deep pink flowers.

'Variegata'. A slow-growing, compact selection with creamy white leaf edges and white flowers. An excellent accent plant for a shaded area of the garden.

Prunus laurocerasus
Cherry laurel

Cherry laurel has lustrous, dark green leaves and white, upright flower stalks in spring. This dense evergreen shrub is a close relative to the deciduous ornamental flowering cherries.

The variety 'Schipkaensis' is a common selection with thin, long leaves and a wide-spreading growth habit. Established plants can grow 5–6 ft. high with twice the width. 'Otto Luyken' is a more compact variety, growing 3–4 ft. tall and 6–8 ft. wide. Both varieties are very effective in mass plantings or small

groupings in a shade garden. They can also be effective as a low screen or informal hedge. Cut branches are excellent additions to a holiday floral display. This shrub has an unmistakable presence in the winter landscape, with its glossy foliage and layered growth habit.

Cherry laurel prefers shade and will perform admirably in partial or dense shade. Cherry laurel also thrives in moist, well-drained, acidic, organic soil. Excessive pruning should be avoided since this can ruin cherry laurel's spreading growth habit. Selective pruning can be done in early spring, while the plants are still dormant, or modest maintenance pruning can be performed right after flowering. Hardy from Zones 6–8.

Rhododendron spp.
Rhododendron

Although rhododendrons are highly prized flowering shrubs offering masses of colorful blossoms in spring and summer, they can also provide ornamental value long after the flowers have faded. Even in winter, rhododendrons brighten up the garden with lush, evergreen foliage and dense growth patterns.

Rhododendrons are known as ericaceous plants, which means they are in the Ericaceae family and have specific cultural requirements. These needs include moist, acidic (pH of about 55), organic, well-drained soils, and partial shade. Rhododendrons offer a wide variety of landscape uses and are most effective in mass plantings, foundation plantings, and in shade gardens.

Yak rhododendron foliage

While there are hundreds of species that grow around the world, one of the most beautiful is the yak, or yako, rhododendron (*Rhododendron yakushimanum*). It is a Japanese native and has a compact growth habit and lush green leaves. The undersides of the leaves, new growth, and stems are covered with a soft, felty coating called indumentum. This soft texture contrasts well with the glossy green leaf surface. In spring, the rosy pink flower buds open to medium or pale pink and later fade to white. Yak rhododendron is a wonderful addition to a small garden with limited space. Several varieties such as 'Ken Janek', 'Yaku Princess', and 'Fantastica' are yak hybrids. Hardy from Zones 5–7.

The rhododendrons listed below are great additions to the landscape. They are generally hardy from Zones 4–7, though that may vary depending on the specific species or variety. These are spring bloomers that also offer excellent foliage and dense evergreen habit. At the end of each variety description, minimum hardiness zones are listed.

NOTABLE VARIETIES

'Aglo'. A medium-sized plant with bright pink flowers and small, dark green leaves. Zone 4.

'Anita Gehnrich'. This mid-spring bloomer has showy deep pink flowers fading to a paler shade of pink. The dark green, lustrous leaves and mounded, dense growth habit are also very attractive. Zone 5.

'Fantastica'. Dark green foliage makes a wonderful backdrop to showy, bright pink flowers in spring.

'Ken Janek'. A wonderful selection with a dwarf, mounded growth habit and soft pink spring flowers. The undersides of the leaves have a soft, felty texture that adds a nice contrast to the leaves. Zone 5.

'Percy Wiseman'. A beautiful, mounded shrub with flowers offering shades of pink, yellow, and creamy white. The habit is dense and mounded, and foliage is dark green. Zone 6.

'PJM'. An old favorite with bright purple flowers and an upright growth habit. The glossy green leaves turn deep maroon in the winter. Zone 4.

'Scintillation'. This variety offers large, lush, glossy green foliage and showy clear pink flowers in spring. Zone 5.

'Solidarity'. Large, bold, pink flowers have a light purplish pink throat. Plant habit is dense and mound-

Large red flower buds of 'Taurus'

ed when young, becoming large and open over time. Zone 5.

'Taurus'. In early spring, the stunning, large, deep red flowers stand out against the deep green foliage. Before the flowers open, the dark, purplish red flower buds offer winter interest. Zone 6.

'Yaku Princess'. Purplish-pink flowers contrast well with the attractive, dark green foliage. The undersides of the leaves also have a soft, dark orange-yellow coloration. A very compact, dense, rounded habit. Zone 5.

{ *Skimmia japonica*
Japanese skimmia

This beautiful, low-growing shrub will grow 3–4 ft. tall with a similar spread. The small, glossy, green leaves form a dense mat of growth. This Asian species is dioecious, with male and female flowers borne on separate plants. The flowers are deep red maroon to greenish white in bud, opening to creamy white in flower. Male flower clusters are larger than female flowers, but once pollinated, the female plants will display bunches of bright red, holly-like fruit the entire winter season. The attractive fruit clusters nestled around the dark, lustrous green foliage is quite handsome.

Skimmia prefers moist, well-drained acidic soil and partial shade. It is extremely adaptable to dense shade. Protection from windy, exposed sites is also beneficial.

Skimmia is a great companion plant to rhododendrons, azaleas, mountain laurel, and pieris and can be used in groupings, foundation plantings, and shade gardens along the edge of a path. It is somewhat obscure and difficult to find commercially, but is well worth the effort of acquisition for the home garden. Hardy from Zones 6–9 but needs special care and siting in Zones 6 and 9.

{ *Trochodendron aralioides*
Wheel tree

Wheel tree is a close relative of English ivy and inherited its name from the wheellike, circular pattern of the foliage and flower clusters. This rather obscure species has attractive deep green foliage, and its bold

Male flowers of Japanese skimmia

Wheel tree's circular foliage pattern

texture will stand out in the landscape. The growth habit is upright and narrow, growing 10–20 ft. tall at maturity.

Wheel tree prefers moist, well-drained soil and partial shade in a protected location. It is very tolerant of shade and will add interest as a specimen plant in a woodland setting. Hardy from Zones 6–7.

Wheel tree is a specialty item for the collector and will add character to the winter landscape. It should be sited in a noticeable area of the garden and will become a focal point as it matures.

Viburnum spp.
Evergreen viburnums

During the winter, certain species and varieties of deciduous viburnums will offer interesting fruit that will catch the garden enthusiast's eye. But evergreen viburnums will also offer versatility and beauty to the landscape. The superb leaf texture makes a bold statement in the winter landscape even while the shrubs lie dormant. Evergreen viburnums are very effective as screens, informal hedges, and in mass plantings. Below are a few types of evergreen viburnums suitable for the home landscape.

Viburnum x *burkwoodii* (Burkwood viburnum)

This semi-evergreen species has dark, glossy, green leaves most of the year. In harsh winters some or all of the foliage may drop due to extended cold temperatures. Burkwood viburnum develops into an upright, open shrub reaching 8–10 ft. high with a slightly smaller spread. In spring, white, rounded flowers will fill the garden with a sweet fragrance. Hardy from Zones 4–8. This plant benefits from protection in Zone 4.

NOTABLE VARIETIES

'Conoy'. This is a truly dwarf variety, with lustrous, glossy leaves and a dense growth habit. It grows to 5–6 ft. high with an equal spread. Because of its compact growth habit, this shrub is ideal for small landscapes and can be used in groupings and foundation plantings. Truly evergreen, its leaves are often tinged with a deep purple color in the winter.

'Eskimo'. This hybrid offers large, white flowers that lack fragrance but exhibit a spectacular display of color in spring, with flower clusters reaching 4–5 in. in diameter.

'Mohawk'. This hybrid viburnum has a dense, rounded growth habit and dark green, lustrous leaves that turn brilliant shades of orange, red, and purple in autumn. This variety holds its leaves late into fall but is deciduous. The red flower buds open to white and provide a sweet, spicy fragrance in spring.

Lustrous foliage of Prague viburnum

Leatherleaf viburnum foliage

Viburnum x *pragense* (Prague viburnum)

The Prague viburnum is one of the most handsome evergreen viburnums. The dark green, glossy, and roughly textured leaves provide interest in the garden year round. The rounded, creamy white flowers emerge in spring and will persist for several weeks. These shrubs can grow up to 10 ft. tall with a similar spread. Occasional selective pruning will keep plants dense and productive. Prague viburnum is very effective as a screening plant, informal hedge, or as a backdrop to smaller plants. It can also be used as a single specimen. Hardy from Zones 5–8.

Viburnum rhytidophyllum (leatherleaf viburnum)

Leatherleaf viburnum offers large, thick, leathery, dark green leaves with a sandpaper-like texture. The large, flat-topped, creamy white flowers open in spring. This coarse-textured plant will grow to 15 ft. high with a similar spread. Leatherleaf viburnum has a distinctive appearance in the landscape and is suitable as a single specimen or in groupings. Hardy from Zones 5–7.

A similar species, lantanaphyllum viburnum (*Viburnum* x *rhytidophylloides*), is a hybrid of leatherleaf viburnum. Lantanaphyllum is semi-evergreen to deciduous, depending on the climate. In milder climates it will typically retain some of its foliage. The leaves are slightly smaller than those of leatherleaf viburnum.

Several varieties provide excellent foliage and flower interest in the landscape. 'Allegheny' has extremely dark green, leathery leaves, white flowers in spring, and bright red fruit that turns black in fall. 'Willowwood' is a durable shrub with beautiful green foliage and arching, graceful branches. Hardy from Zones 5–8. Will also grow in Zone 4 if sited in a sheltered location.

Conifers

A conifer is defined as a tree or shrub bearing cones. In addition to having cones, conifers have thin, needlelike foliage unlike broadleaf evergreens, which have wider leaves. There are many popular conifers, as well as a few lesser-known species, that present fine-textured foliage ranging from rich green to blue-green and great architectural form that is highlighted in the winter landscape. In addition, many species bear interesting cones that can be used for holiday home decorating. Conifers add a unique quality to the landscape that is unlike any other group of plants. Well-developed specimens provide an elegant feature to the garden and enhance everything around them. Although the popular belief is that all conifers are evergreen, such as pine and spruce, some conifers are, in fact, deciduous.

"It is only when the cold season comes that we know the pine and cypress to be evergreens."
—*Chinese proverb*

97

Evergreen Conifers

{ *Abies* spp.
  Fir

Firs and spruces (*Picea* spp.) are similar in their physical appearance and are often confused in the landscape. However, upon closer inspection, these two evergreen genera do have several key differences. Spruce needles are attached to the stems by a small, peglike stalk, which is absent in firs. In addition, spruce cones dangle along the stems and eventually fall to the ground, while fir cones point straight up and shatter when ripe. Fir needles also have two distinct white bands on the underside of their needles.

But besides the up-close physical differences, the growth habit of spruce and fir are quite similar. Both possess an upright, conical habit and several species of spruce can also possess a sweeping, graceful branching pattern. Both spruces and firs are conifers of major significance in our forests and landscapes. Firs and spruces thrive in the cooler climates and higher elevations of North America, Asia, and Europe. They both prefer well-drained, moist soil and full or partial sun.

Firs and spruces can be effectively used as specimens, in groupings, or as living screens. The cut branches are also useful for decorating during the holidays; however, fir greens will typically last longer in an arrangement or display.

There are about forty species of fir that grow all over the world. In general, they are large, pyramidal evergreens that will typically outgrow the small, residential landscape. Some magnificent firs that are often

A beautifully decorated fir wreath

"I began to be exhilarated by the sight of the wild fir and spruce tops, and those of other primitive evergreens, peering through the mist in the horizon. It was like the sight and odor of cake to a schoolboy."
—*Henry David Thoreau*

encountered on large sites such as parks and arboreta include Greek fir (*Abies cephalonica*), Nikko fir (*Abies homolepis*), and Nordmann fir *(Abies nordmanniana)*, just to name a few. Several native firs to North American mountainous regions include Fraser fir (*Abies fraseri*) and balsam fir (*Abies balsamea*). None of these species are particularly suitable for the home garden. However, the two firs listed below are suitable for the residential landscape and are gaining in popularity.

Abies concolor (white fir)

White fir is an interesting conifer with long, smooth, silvery blue needles. The slender, thin needles and soft texture provides a graceful, bright accent in the garden. White fir has a tight, pyramidal growth habit when young and will eventually become tall and broad as it matures. It is a truly breathtaking site in the winter landscape.

Like most firs, this species prefers moist, well-drained soil and full sun or partial shade. White fir is relatively easy to grow and will adapt to many landscape situations. It can grow 30–50 ft. or more in height and should be sited where it will have adequate room to grow.

White fir is useful as a single specimen or in a grouping. It can be used as a screen to block an unsightly view or soften an architectural feature. The silver foliage will brighten up the garden and add beautiful contrast to a green landscape. 'Candicans' has bright silvery blue needles and a distinctly upright growth habit—it looks like a Colorado blue spruce, only better. Hardy from Zones 4–7.

White fir needles

Abies koreana (Korean fir)

This slow-growing evergreen is relatively small in stature with a compact growth habit. The needles are dark green above with two white bands on the undersides. The small, purple cones are 2–3 in. long and can also be quite interesting against the dark green foliage. 'Horstmann's Silverlocke', a popular garden variety, has unusual, curled needles that display beautiful silver bands on the undersides. 'Prostrata' is an unusual, low-growing form that will hug the ground as it grows.

Korean fir is slightly more tolerant of heat and humidity than most firs but performs best in cooler climates. It also prefers moist, well-drained, acidic soils and full sun or partial shade.

'Horstmann's Silverlocke' is an excellent accent plant or conversation piece for the home garden. It will blend in well with other unusual specimens in a collector's garden. It is a great companion plant to other unusual conifers, dwarf flowering shrubs and broadleaf evergreens. Hardy from Zones 5–7.

{ *Cephalotaxus harringtonia*
Plum yew

Plum yew is a very interesting evergreen shrub with narrow, dark green, lustrous leaves similar to yew (*Taxus* spp.). The leaves often form a V-shaped pattern along the stems and are typically not as soft to the touch as yew. This upright, slow-growing evergreen can grow into a small tree, but with so many new varieties available, plum yew can take on many forms in the garden. 'Duke Gardens', which originated in from Duke Gardens in North Carolina, has a dense, spreading habit and will eventually grow to 3 ft. tall and 4 to 5 ft. wide. 'Fastigiata' has a broad, upright growth habit up to 10 ft. tall. 'Prostrata' is a useful groundcover type, only growing 2–3 ft. tall and spreading 3–4 ft. or more.

Plum yew is a remarkably resilient shrub that prefers partial shade and moist, well-drained soil but will also perform reasonably well in drier, sandy soil, heavy clay soil, and full sun or dense shade. Plum yew is generally tougher than *Taxus,* especially in the southeastern United States and will grow where no *Taxus* dares to grow. This Japanese native is quite resistant to most pests, including deer. Plum yew is a slow grower but its low maintenance qualities and durability make it a worthwhile addition to the garden.

Depending on the variety, plum yew can be used in groupings, foundation plantings, rock gardens, on embankments, and as informal hedges and screens. Hardy from Zones 6–9 but will also grow in Zone 5 with protection.

{ *Chamaecyparis* spp.
Falsecypress

Chamaecyparis, also known as falsecypress, is one of the most diverse and ornamental of all the evergreens suited for the home landscape. They form a pyramidal habit and provide a certain elegance that is very recognizable in the landscape. The smooth, scalelike leaves offer a soft texture in a variety of pleasing, eye-catching colors, including emerald green, blue-green, and, gold.

Chamaecyparis obtusa (Hinoki falsecypress)

This distinct evergreen displays wavy sprays of emerald green foliage and a delightfully graceful, mounded growth habit. Mature specimens will also exhibit a flaking, reddish brown bark. Although this conifer is slow growing, it can easily grow 30 ft. or more tall and will outgrow a small, residential landscape. However, the varieties 'Nana' and 'Nana Gracilis' are extremely slow-growing forms, reaching only 3–6 ft.

Hinoki falsecypress

Weeping nootka falsecypress with its drooping lateral branches

high, which is ideal for a small garden.

Hinoki falsecypress thrives in well-drained, rich, acidic soil and full sun or partial shade. This delicate plant should not be exposed to heavy winds, pollution, or poor, infertile soils. Pruning should be kept to a minimum since excessive pruning will compromise its beautiful, natural form.

Hinoki falsecypress is very effective along the foundation of a house, in groupings, or as a single specimen. It can also be grown in ornamental containers and urns. Hardy from Zones 5–8.

Chamaecyparis nootkatensis 'Pendula' (weeping nootka falsecypress)

This upright conifer has striking blue-green foliage

and a weeping growth habit. The main trunk of the tree grows upward, while the lateral branches hang toward the ground. This delicate, drooping habit is very picturesque, especially as it sways on a windy winter day.

Like most *Chamaecyparis*, weeping nootka falsecypress performs best in full sun or partial shade and moist, well-drained soil. It is a stand-alone plant in the landscape and is a very effective specimen in a highly visible area of the garden. Hardy from Zones 4–8.

Chamaecyparis thyoides (Atlantic white cedar)

This evergreen tree is native to the east coast of the United States and is typically found in swampy, lowland areas. This species is not widely available, but several new and exciting dwarf or semi-dwarf varieties have emerged. These dwarf varieties are useful in groupings, foundation plantings, or as companion plants to other dwarf conifers and flowering plants.

'Heatherbun' has a tight, rounded, compact habit to 4 ft. tall with an equal spread and soft, blue-green foliage that turns plum color in winter. 'Red Star' offers blue-green foliage that turns deep green to plum in winter. It has a tight, columnar growth habit and will eventually reach 15–25 ft. tall. 'Shiva' is an interesting variety with beautiful green, feathery foliage and a pyramidal growth habit.

The cultivated varieties of Atlantic white cedar prefer moist soils but will tolerate drier conditions once established. Sandy or well-drained, moist garden soils are best, but this adaptable evergreen is quite tolerant of various soil types. Full sun is best, but it will tolerate partial shade as well. Hardy from Zones 4–8 and possibly 9 with some additional care and specific siting.

Cedrus spp.
True cedars

Arborvitae, juniper, and falsecypress are sometimes referred to as red or white cedar because of their cedar-like bark and wood. However, none of these trees are true cedars. While common names can often be misleading, the conifers within the genus *Cedrus* are known as the true cedars. Because of its strength and durability, cedar wood is ideal for structural timber. As ornamentals, atlas cedar (*Cedrus atlantica*), deodara cedar (*Cedrus deodara*), and cedar of Lebanon (*Cedrus libani*) are the three true

cedars with sharp, green needles and wide-spreading growth habits. Cedars also have large, egg-shaped female cones reaching 3–5 in. long that develop on the upper half of the tree. After two years, the cones ripen and shatter, sprinkling the ground with small, brown scales. Deodar cedar is quite prevalent in the southern states, while atlas cedar and cedar of Lebanon are found primarily in northern gardens.

Although cedars develop into large, upright trees over 50 ft. tall, given the proper room to grow they will be admired for many years as graceful, majestic focal points

> "It was evening all afternoon.
> It was snowing
> And it was going to snow.
> The blackbird sat
> In the cedar limbs."
> —*Wallace Stevens*

in the landscape. They are not suitable or small, residential landscapes with limited space. Atlas cedar and the popular garden variety known as blue atlas cedar (*Cedrus atlantica* 'Glauca') will establish quickly in the landscape and eventually form a rounded, dense growth habit. The short, stout needles and long, elegant horizontal branches are particularly beautiful in the winter landscape. The variety 'Pendula' has long, weeping branches that cascade to the ground like a beautiful waterfall. Deodar cedar has longer, more delicate needles and a pyramidal, open growth habit

Vincent A. Simeone

Deodar cedar in snow

that is also quite striking. The variety 'Kashmir' has blue-green foliage and is slightly hardier then the species. Cedar of Lebanon has a distinctly pyramidal growth habit with horizontally layered lateral branches. Established specimens become stately over time.

All three of these species grow into beautifully sculpted evergreens as they mature. During the winter months, ice and snow will collect on their strong, layered branches making them even more noticeable in the landscape. A single specimen or a grouping of three is equally effective in an open lawn area.

Cedars prefer moist, well-drained, soil and full sun but adapt well to varying soils and partial shade. Atlas cedar is hardy from Zones 6–9, while deodar cedar is hardy from Zones 7–9. Cedar of Lebanon is hardy from Zones 5–7.

Atlas cedar in a winter wonderland

Weeping blue atlas cedar trained as an archway

{ *Cryptomeria japonica*
Japanese cryptomeria

Japanese cryptomeria is an upright, dense conifer with short, medium-green, needlelike leaves spirally arranged along extended, thin stems. In the winter, the leaves will change to a bronzy color until spring. Established specimens will display a peeling, reddish brown cedarlike bark. Japanese cryptomeria can grow 50 ft. or taller but are typically found in the 30–40 ft. range in the landscape.

Japanese cryptomeria prefers moist, well-drained, acidic soil and full sun or partial shade. Pruning should be kept to a minimum and should only be done to remove dead twigs or leaves. Occasional pruning may be done to train this plant as a dense tall hedge or screen.

Cryptomeria is an excellent specimen tree that is also very useful in groupings and as a screen. It can easily be used in the same manner as hemlock, arborvitae, and falsecypress. Hardy from Zones 5–8.

The most popular variety is 'Yoshino' with rich green leaves. The bright green color persists into the winter although leaves may be slightly tinged with a bronze hue.

{ *Cupressus arizonica*
Arizona cypress

This unusual conifer has blue-green foliage; interesting rounded cones; a sturdy, upright growth habit; and reddish brown bark. It is fast growing and will establish quickly in a sunny area of the garden. Arizona cypress can grow over 40 ft. tall and 25 ft. wide, so you should give it ample room to grow.

Like other relatives of juniper, this species does best in full sun and well-drained soil. The variety 'Blue Ice' has silvery blue foliage that is stunning in all four seasons. This lightly colored, icy blue foliage contrasts well with the mahogany red stems. The growth habit of 'Blue Ice' is dense and conical. Because of these ornamental characteristics, Arizona cypress is an effective accent plant, single specimen, screening plant, or in an informal grouping. I have also seen this plant thriving in large containers in an urban setting and performing admirably. Hardy from Zones 7–9.

{ *Juniperus* spp.
Juniper

While junipers are generally regarded as overused shrubs these days, it is hard to exclude them when discussing the winter landscape. Junipers come in all shapes, colors, and sizes and will tolerate heat,

Textured bark of the eastern red cedar

drought, cold, pollution, and poor soil. But while there are dozens of species and hundreds of varieties, a native species, eastern red cedar (*Juniperus virginiana*), is one of the most versatile, functional, and aesthetically pleasing. This fast-growing and adaptable evergreen has an upright conical growth habit and dark green foliage. It is widely distributed throughout eastern and central North America and will grow just about anywhere in the landscape.

Eastern red cedar can grow into a medium or large tree, to 50 ft. tall, and as it matures it develops a handsome, reddish brown or gray bark that sheds in long strips. The wood of this tree has a reddish pink color and aromatic scent. Often the deep green foliage turns a bronzy purple during the winter months.

Eastern red cedar thrives in sandy, well-drained soil and full sun. However, I have observed it growing in partial shade and heavy soils as well. It is very effective in groupings along the seashore or in a very exposed, hot, dry area of the landscape. It can also be used as a screening plant or as a single specimen in a cultivated garden setting. The lower limbs of mature trees can be removed to expose the beautiful bark, which is especially noticeable in the winter landscape. Hardy from Zones 3–9.

{ *Picea* spp.
Spruce

There are many species and varieties of spruce that will thrive under the right conditions and serve various landscape functions. Although common species such as Colorado blue spruce are overused and often misused, here are a few alternatives that will enhance the winter landscape. Please note that although the species presented in the text may grow too large for small landscapes, the garden varieties listed are more appropriate for residential sites.

Picea abies (Norway spruce)

Norway spruce is a large, pyramidal conifer with long, sweeping branches and an elegant growth habit.

The dark green needles and graceful, dense growth habit can add a nice backdrop to a garden in winter. This attractive evergreen can easily reach 60 ft. or more in height and must be given adequate space to grow. As the tree matures, the lower limbs arch down to the ground in a sweeping pattern.

While Norway spruce is best suited for large, commercial sites, several dwarf forms—including 'Clanbrassiliana', 'Maxwellii', and 'Nidiformis'—are appropriate for a home garden. 'Nidiformis' forms a tight, spreading habit 3–5 ft. tall and wide and can be used as a foundation plant, companion plant to other dwarf shrubs, or in a rock garden. 'Clanbrassiliana' and 'Maxwellii' are slow-growing selections that form dense mounds, under 10 ft. tall, in the landscape. 'Pendula' is a peculiar looking form with the main trunk and side branches of the tree weeping to the ground like a cascading waterfall.

Norway spruce and its varieties prefer full sun and well-drained, acidic soils with moderate moisture. Plants will tolerate partial shade and poor, rocky soils as well. One of the most desirable attributes of Norway spruce is that, a native of Europe, it has adapted exceptionally well to North American climates. It is an excellent and adaptable species that thrives in cool climates and performs exceptionally well in warm climates.

Norway spruce can be used as a specimen, in groupings, or as a screening plant. If the dwarf varieties are not used, careful site selection is important to ensure the large-growing, straight species will not overwhelm your landscape. Performs best in Zones 3–7.

Picea omorika (Serbian spruce)

Serbian spruce is an upright, narrow-growing evergreen with dark green needles that have white bands on the undersides. Often the tips of the branches are noticeably accented with a bluish white coloration. The main trunk is particularly vertical, with the lateral branches short and arching. Mature specimens develop a distinctly vertical and graceful habit in the landscape, creating a very striking architectural outline, especially noticeable in winter.

Serbian spruce can grow 50 ft. or more in height but only 20 ft. wide; therefore, it can be used in garden areas where overhead space is available but there is limited width. 'Nana' is a dwarf variety with a densely conical or rounded growth habit that will reach only 8–10 ft. high. 'Pendula' is a very unusual looking variety, with a tall, slender main trunk and beautiful, short weeping side branches. This graceful conifer is an excellent specimen tree and can also be used effectively in small groupings. It is undoubtedly one of the most elegant conifers for the plant collector.

Serbian spruce performs best in full sun or partial shade and in moist, rich, well-drained soil. This spruce should not be planted in highly exposed, windy sites. It is an extremely adaptable and cold-hardy tree, thriving in Zones 4–7.

Picea orientalis (Oriental spruce)

Oriental spruce is without a doubt one of the most spectacular conifers for the garden. Few trees rival the beauty of this graceful conifer. The short, glossy, dark green needles, pyramidal habit, and sweeping branches provide a four-season attraction. Oriental spruce will also display small cones, which are purple when young and eventually turn brown when mature. This elegant evergreen is a focal point in the garden, especially in winter when it glistens on a sunny day.

Dark green needles and cones of Oriental spruce

Golden yellow foliage of 'Skylands' Oriental spruce

Although Oriental spruce does not grow quite as fast as other spruces, such as Norway and Colorado, it is well worth the wait. I have never been disappointed with any specimen of Oriental spruce that I have encountered in the landscape. Oriental spruce adapts well to various soils and light exposures but thrives in full sun and well-drained, moist soil. It will tolerate rocky soils but does not like arid or excessively cold environments. Like Norway spruce, this species will grow into a large specimen, so careful siting is essential. 'Gowdy' is a compact variety with a dense, narrow habit reaching 8–10 ft. tall. 'Nana' is a globular, low-growing variety that only grows a few feet tall and wide. 'Skylands' is an interesting form with bright golden yellow needles that will add a nice splash of color to a green landscape.

Oriental spruce is truly one of the most beautiful trees in the winter landscape. While it is spectacular all year, the winter seems to bring out the best in this wonderful landscape treasure. Oriental spruce is ideal as a single specimen, screen, or in groupings. On my top-fifteen list of favorite trees, this is easily number one! Hardy from Zones 4–7.

{ *Pinus* spp. Pine

Pines are a very diverse and widely used group of trees that are prominent fixtures in the winter landscape. The soft, fine texture of the needles, intriguing bark, and dense growth habit are three important ornamental characteristics possessed by pine. While there are many to choose from, here are a few choice species worth serious consideration.

Pinus bungeana (lacebark pine)

The lacebark pine has an interesting upright growth habit and dark, thick glossy green needles. But the most interesting attribute of this plant is the multicolored, exfoliating bark that displays shades of green, tan, brown, and white. Established trees can be effective as a single specimen or in small groupings. Mature specimens will reach 30–50 ft. tall and 20–30

Shiny bark of lacebark pine

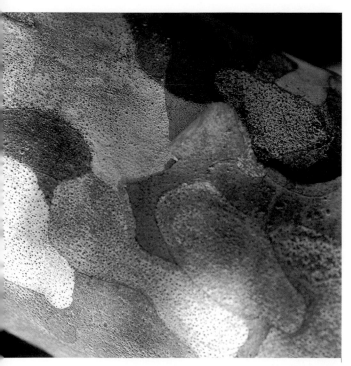
Multicolored bark of lacebark pine

of the habit are very handsome. It is a wonderful specimen tree for a woodland setting amongst rhododendrons and other broadleaf evergreens. It can also be featured in a lawn area in full sun. Mature specimens can range from 25–40 ft. tall with a similar spread. Hardy from Zones 4–7.

Pinus strobus (eastern white pine)

White pine is one of the most popular native pines, growing from Canada to the southeastern and midwestern United States. Its flexible, blue-green foliage is very soft to the touch. Although this conifer will develop into a large, magnificent tree, eastern white pine will get too large for the average garden—mature specimens reaching 60 ft. and greater. However, there are several varieties that are appropriate for the home landscape. 'Compacta' is a slow-growing dense form that will eventually reach 8–10 ft. high with an equal spread. It can be used as a single specimen or in groupings strategically placed in the landscape. 'Pendula' is a very interesting selection with the main trunk and side branches weeping toward the ground, creating an interesting graceful appearance with age. It is typically used as a single specimen that can be viewed from all sides.

Eastern white pine grows best in deep, rich, acidic soil and full sun or partial shade. It needs adequate moisture and protection from harsh winds. This soft-wooded tree is often damaged by high winds and heavy snow and ice accumulations. Hardy from Zones 3–8.

ft. wide. This choice species is tolerant of drought, pests, and various soil types. Although it prefers sun, lacebark pine is very adaptable to shade. Hardy from Zones 4–7. Lacebark pine should be sited in a sheltered location in Zone 4. This is truly one of the most care-free and beautiful conifers available.

Pinus parviflora (Japanese white pine)

Japanese white pine is an irregular growing, medium-sized pine with blue-green foliage. The short, soft, blue-green needles and picturesque character

Vincent A. Simeone

Weeping white pine

Umbrella pine's unique pattern of leaves

Pinus wallichiana (Himalayan pine) and P. koraiensis (Korean pine)

Two species that are closely related to eastern white pine that can also add great interest to the winter landscape are the Himalayan pine (*Pinus wallichiana*) and Korean pine (*Pinus koraiensis*). The Himalayan pine has beautiful semi-pendulous branches and long drooping needles. The graceful growth habit and blue-green, softly textured needles make this a showpiece in the landscape. 'Zebrina' is a striking variegated selection with yellow-striped foliage. Korean pine has dense, stout tufts of growth that have a distinct bluish green color. This impressive color is especially noticeable in the stark winter landscape.

Sciadopitys verticillata
Japanese umbrella pine

Japanese umbrella pine is a unique and beautiful conifer that will undoubtedly stand out in the landscape. The slender, dark green leaves radiate around the stems in a circular pattern. The strong, pyramidal growth habit, dense branching habit, and shedding, reddish brown bark are also admirable ornamental qualities. Foliage usually hides the bark unless the tree's lower limbs are removed. Mature specimens can easily grow to 30 ft. tall and develop a distinctive and very handsome habit once established.

Reddish brown peeling bark of yew

Japanese umbrella pine is a slow-growing tree that prefers full sun or partial shade and moist, well-drained, acidic soils. Regular pruning is not needed and is only necessary if a broken or damaged branch is in need of attention.

Japanese umbrella pine is ideal as a single specimen in an open lawn area. It is especially noticeable in the winter, when it stands out against the bare landscape. 'Jim Cross' is a dwarf variety named after the late, great nurseryman from Environmentals Nursery in Long Island, New York. 'Ossorio Gold' and 'Aurea' are

two golden forms with striking yellow foliage that provide attractive accents to the landscape. Hardy from Zones 5–7.

{ *Taxus* spp.
Yew

Yews are very popular evergreens that have a variety of landscape applications, including formal and informal hedges, screens, and foundation plantings. Yews are prized landscape shrubs because they remain green year-round, are easy to grow, and tolerate a wide range of environmental conditions. Very often yews are found in the landscape pruned unmercifully to create tight boxes, rounded gumdrop shapes, or any number of other unnatural forms. The Hicks yew (*Taxus* × *media* 'Hicksii') is most often used for formal hedges. But if left unpruned, yews can mature into wonderful, wide-spreading specimen trees.

Yews offer dark, finely textured, needlelike foliage, red fleshy covered seeds (not edible) in summer, and stunning reddish brown bark that peels with age. The interesting bark is more obvious on established specimens that are of considerable size. The broad, spreading, or upright habit and densely arranged branches produce strong figures in the winter landscape. Yew wood is very durable, and legend has it that Robin Hood used the branches of the yew for bows. Yews have a storied history in Europe, where specimens dating back thousands of years can still be found living in Scotland and England. Yew also has medicinal value, and a compound known as Taxol has been developed from a West Coast species of

Taxus to treat certain types of cancer. Foliage, bark, and seeds can be poisonous to humans and animals if ingested.

Yews generally prefer moist, acidic, well-drained soil but will also tolerate high pH soils. Yews will thrive in sandy loam soils but do not perform well in heavy, poorly drained soils since root rots and other pests can cause problems. Full sun is preferable, but yews are remarkably tolerant of shady conditions. The lower limbs on older specimens can be removed to expose the beautiful bark. Yew foliage can suffer winter burn from cold, desiccating winds but will normally recover in spring.

There are several species of *Taxus* commonly found commercially, but the two best for winter interest are the Japanese yew (*T. cuspidata*) and the English yew (*T. baccata*). Japanese yew has medium to dark green leaves and peeling, reddish brown bark. It will grow upright or spread and can reach 20–40 ft. tall at maturity. The garden variety 'Nana' is a slow-growing and mounded form that reaches 10 ft. or more tall.

English Yew has extremely dark green foliage and a treelike habit, growing 30 ft. or more tall with a slightly smaller spread. The exfoliating, reddish brown bark is especially striking on older plants. The variety 'Repandens' is a low, mounded form with cascading branches. Mature specimens typically reach 2–4 ft. tall and twice as wide. This form has a very distinct, semi-weeping habit. Conversely, the variety 'Fastigiata' has a columnar shape; mature specimens grow 20–30 ft. tall and only 4–8 ft. wide. English yew is hardy from Zones 5–7, while Japanese yew is slightly more cold hardy, growing from Zones 4–7.

'Atrovirens' western arborvitae as a screen

{ *Thuja* spp.
Arborvitae

Arborvitae, also known as the "tree of life," is a popular landscape evergreen that has been an integral part of the American landscape for decades. American arborvitae (*Thuja occidentalis*) is a very common and overused evergreen that is found in many commercial and residential landscapes across the United States. However, western arborvitae (*Thuja plicata*) is a lesser-known species and superior alternative. This beautiful evergreen tree has a pyramidal, graceful growth habit and smooth, emerald green leaves that look good all year round. This tree can grow quite large and must be sited in areas of the garden where it can freely grow. There are several excellent garden varieties that are wonderful additions to the landscape. 'Atrovirens' is a common variety with deep green foliage and an open pyramidal habit. It can be used as a single specimen or tall screen. As it matures, it creates an impenetrable mass of foliage. 'Virescens' is another choice variety with a tight conical habit and blue-green foliage. This variety is suitable for areas of the garden where space is limited.

Western arborvitae is an extremely adaptable evergreen that tolerates poor soils, varying soil pH, wind, drought, and other adverse conditions. During the winter months, it is quite durable to the damaging weight of snow and desiccating winds. It is also very tolerant of light exposure and, although western arborvitae thrives in sun, it is also very shade tolerant. Thrives in moist, well-drained soil.

Since western arborvitae can reach 50 ft. tall and 30 ft. wide at maturity, it should be given plenty of room. However, it can be kept under control with regular and judicious pruning. It is an excellent single specimen or can be used in a grouping to create a dense screen. It is a superb replacement for native species such as Canadian hemlock that have been decimated by pest problems in the northeastern United States. It is also a much better landscape tree than Leyland cypress, an overused and fast-growing evergreen tree. Hardy from Zones 4–8.

'Atrovirens' foliage

Deciduous Conifers

In addition to evergreen conifers, there are several unique conifers that shed their leaves in the fall and regain them in the spring. Among these select specimen trees are the dawn redwood, the golden larch, and the bald cypress.

Metasequoia glyptostroboides Dawn redwood

The dawn redwood is a living testimony to the treasures produced by nature. Fossil evidence proved that this tree was abundant when dinosaurs roamed the earth. Once native to North America, it was thought to have been absent from the continent for 15 million years. This magnificent tree was believed to be extinct until the 1940s, when it was discovered growing in a remote valley of the Szechwan province in China. Seed was brought to the Arnold Arboretum in Boston, Massachusetts, where it was eventually distributed across the country.

Dawn redwood is in the same family as the California redwoods that reach great heights in nature but, unlike California redwood, it drops its leaves in the autumn. The soft, fernlike leaves are medium green during the summer, turning various shades of orange, reddish brown, or bronze in fall. The narrowly growing conical shape and beautiful, rusty brown, peeling, redwood-like bark is quite attractive in the winter. Unusual depressions, also called "armpits," form where the lateral branches connect to the main trunk of the tree. As the tree

Dawn redwood bark with "armpits"

Vincent A. Simeone

Golden larch (left) and yew (right) in winter

matures, the base of the trunk becomes swollen and pronounced.

Although dawn redwood is a fast grower, reaching heights of 100 ft. or more, it typically only grows 25 ft. wide. It thrives in moist, rich, well-drained soil and full sun or partial shade. Regular pruning is not usually needed, and trees should be left to grow naturally. Dawn redwood has a natural beauty and grace that provides four seasons of interest.

Because of dawn redwood's ultimate size, it should be sited in a visible and spacious area of the garden, such as a lawn area. Dawn redwood may also have value as a street tree, on wide streets where there is plenty of room and no obstructions such as overhead power lines. Dawn redwood is a truly lovely specimen when it matures. Hardy from Zones 4–8.

{ *Pseudolarix amabilis*
{ Golden larch

Golden larch is another deciduous conifer that displays beauty all year long. Although it is mostly known for its lacy, needled foliage that turns brilliant shades of golden yellow in fall, the upright growth habit with wide-spreading horizontal branches becomes quite attractive with age. Upon close inspection, short, spurlike buds display small annual growth rings, which become most obvious in the winter.

Golden larch is a moderate- to slow-growing tree that can mature to 50 ft. tall. Like dawn redwood, this choice conifer should be sited in a large, open area of the garden where it will receive plenty of sunlight and

Bald cypress "knees"

ample room to grow. For best results, soil should be well drained, rich, acidic, and moist. It is also adaptable to partial shade.

Golden larch is an excellent specimen tree and also can be used in groupings in a lawn area. Although this tree is at its best in the autumn, it is also very attractive in the winter. Hardy from Zones 4–7.

Taxodium distichum
Bald cypress

Bald cypress is a similar deciduous conifer to dawn redwood but is native to the southeastern and midwestern United States. It can be found growing natu-rally in swampy, wet regions of the landscape and is sometimes found in the cultivated garden. Although it looks similar to dawn redwood, bald cypress tends to have a tighter, more narrow growth habit and is slower growing. Most important, unlike dawn red-wood, in wet areas bald cypress will develop "knees", which are bizarre looking wooden spikes that stand straight up around the base of the tree. These knees are interesting all year but especially during the win-ter when there is no foliage to hide them. It is most effective in a grove along a stream or pond. Hardy from Zones 4–11.

Caring for Evergreens

APPENDIX 1

As a general rule, evergreens require even soil moisture and are more likely to be damaged by cold winter temperatures and desiccating winds than are deciduous plants. Although deciduous shrubs can also be effected by heat and drought stress during the summer months, they are not usually susceptible to the same winter damage as evergreens since they shed their leaves in the fall. Even though evergreens are essentially dormant in winter, they can still experience water loss through their leaves on warm, sunny days. The combination of the harsh or fluctuating winter temperatures and drying winds can cause winter burn. For this reason it is important that in regions of the country where extended periods of severe cold temperatures are experienced extra care is taken to protect your plants.

It is important that evergreens are well watered as they go dormant in the autumn season. Stressed plants are more vulnerable and may be severely damaged or killed by the severe extremes of winter. Whether newly installed or established, drought-stressed plants should received a thorough, deep watering prior to the onset of the cold winter temperatures. Mulching trees and shrubs with 1–2 in. of wood chips, pine straw, shredded leaves, or compost will also protect their roots.

Evergreens can be fertilized with a balanced fertilizer such as 10-6-4 or 5-10-5. There are many fertilizer formulations on the market, so check with your local garden center or nursery professional for proper selection of a fertilizer for your specific situation. Also, new plantings should be given several months (a full season) to establish before being put on a regular fertilizer program. If fertilizer is necessary, it should be applied between fall and early spring, while plants are dormant. Before any fertilizer is applied, a soil test should be taken to evaluate the specific needs of the soil. Soil samples can be taken to your local county extension agent for testing.

Winter desiccation can also be a problem with evergreens even if there is adequate moisture in the soil. During the winter, cold or frozen soils make it difficult for roots to absorb and translocate water to leaves and stems. This causes the leaves to dry up, and the surface of the leaf will have a burned appearance. When evergreen leaves wilt in the winter, it is a protective measure to conserve water that is not readily available.

To reduce winter stress on plants, anti-desiccants can be applied to evergreen trees and shrubs to reduce water loss and leaf damage. These anti-desiccants will form a waxy, protective layer on the surface of the leaf and are especially beneficial to broadleaf evergreens. Application of an anti-desiccant is usually done during the late fall or early winter months, although some products can also be used in the summer to reduce drought and heat stress. These products should not be applied when air temperatures are below freezing. It is important to consult your local county extension agent, garden center, or nursery professional before using these products. Also, it is imperative that before using these products you read the directions on the label. Anti-desiccants should only be applied to certain species and varieties of plants. For example, if applied to plants with blue foliage, such as Colorado blue spruce, the needles will turn green.

In addition to using anti-desiccants, there are other ways to protect plants in winter. Wrapping plants with burlap and twine will protect them from wind, ice, and snow. Heavy snow loads can break or bend branches and cause severe physical damage. By tying branches close together, extra support is given to the entire plant to withstand the harsh elements of winter.

Deer-resistant Plants

APPENDIX 2

Deer can be devastating visitors to the garden, defoliating the landscape like a swarm of locusts. Prized trees and shrubs can be ruined overnight, and some plants such as pine, spruce, arborvitae, and juniper often do not recover. Mature trees can be transformed into lollipops with all of the bottom branches defoliated, leaving foliage only on the top half of the tree. Deer feeding on plants is also referred to as "browsing." This browsing is most evident on evergreens and can be especially damaging during the winter, when plants are dormant.

Although deer can potentially browse any plant, there are certain plants that tend to be less appealing to them under normal conditions. However, in harsh winters where much of the landscape is under ice and snow and food is scarce, deer may forage on any plant material they can find. While there are various deer repellents and elaborate fences on the market to protect your garden, the following chart lists a few deer-resistant woody plants that are less likely to be devoured by deer. Please refer to the key to determine the level of attractiveness deer have to a particular plant species.

Plant	Level of Attractiveness
Abies concolor (white fir)	O
Acer griseum (paperbark maple)	O
Aesculus parviflora (bottlebrush buckeye)	S
Aucuba japonica 'Variegata' (gold dust plant)	R
Berberis julianae (wintergreen barberry)	R
Betula papyrifera (paper birch)	R
Carpinus betulus (European hornbeam)	R
Cedrus atlantica (atlas cedar)	R
Cephalotaxus harringtonia (plum yew)	S
Chamaecyparis obtusa (falsecypress)	R
Cornus kousa (kousa dogwood)	S
Cornus sericea (redosier dogwood)	S
Cryptomeria japonica (Japanese cryptomeria)	S
Fagus sylvatica (European beech)	S
Ilex glabra (inkberry holly)	S
Ilex opaca (American holly)	S
Juniperus virginiana (eastern red cedar)	O
Kalmia latifolia (mountain laurel)	S
Leucothoe fontanesiana (drooping leucothoe)	S
Mahonia bealei (leatherleaf mahonia)	S
Picea abies (Norway spruce)	S
Pieris japonica (Japanese pieris)	R
Platanus occidentalis (American sycamore)	R
Salix matsudana (hankow willow)	S
Skimmia japonica (Japanese skimmia)	S
Stewartia pseudocamellia (Japanese stewartia)	S

KEY
R = Rarely Attractive
S = Seldom Attractive
O = Occasionally Attractive

Vinnie's Top Fifteen

APPENDIX 3

Although I admire many trees and shrubs, below is a listing of my top fifteen favorites. These woody plants offer multiple seasons of interest, adaptability, relatively easy culture, and excellent landscape function.

1. Oriental spruce (*Picea orientalis*)
2. Japanese stewartia (*Stewartia pseudocamellia*)
3. Linden viburnum (*Viburnum dilatatum*)
4. Lacebark pine (*Pinus bungeana*)
5. Bottlebrush buckeye (*Aesculus parviflora*)
6. Paperbark maple (*Acer griseum*)
7. Persian parrotia (*Parrotia persica*)
8. European beech (*Fagus sylvatica*)
9. White oak (*Quercus alba*)
10. Flowering dogwood (*Cornus florida*)
11. Western arborvitae (*Thuja plicata*)
12. Japanese clethra (*Clethra barbinervis*)
13. 'Hally Jolivette' cherry (*Prunus* 'Hally Jolivette')
14. Winterberry holly (*Ilex verticillata*)
15. Dawn redwood (*Metasequoia glyptostroboides*)

Enjoying the Sanctuary of a Greenhouse in Winter

APPENDIX 4

While most of us do not have the space or resources to build a greenhouse, glass houses in public and private gardens can provide a wonderful, albeit temporary, haven from the chill of winter. There are many great gardens across the country that are open to the public and feature beautiful outdoor winter landscapes. Many of these gardens also offer amazing greenhouse collections and conservatory structures that will warm the heart and feed the garden soul craving a sign of spring. Here are a few excellent recommendations for winter sanctuaries that will help you in your quest to discover the wonders of the winter landscape.

Atlanta Botanical Garden, Atlanta, Georgia: http://www.atlantabotanicalgarden.org
Brooklyn Botanic Garden, Brooklyn, New York: http://bbg.org
Chicago Botanic Garden, Glencoe, Illinois: http://www.chicagobotanic.org
Cornell Plantations, Ithaca, New York: http://www.plantations.cornell.edu/collections/botanical/winter.cfm
Gardens of Duke Farm, Somerville, New Jersey: http://www.njskylands.com/atdukgar.htm
Lewis Ginter Botanical Garden, Richmond, Virginia: http://www.lewisginter.org
Longwood Gardens, Kennett Square, Pennsylvania: http://www.longwoodgardens.org
Missouri Botanical Garden, St. Louis, Missouri: http://www.mobot.org
Mount Auburn Cemetery, Cambridge, Massachusetts: http://www.mountauburn.org
New York Botanical Garden, Bronx, New York: http://nybg.org
Phipps Conservatory and Botanical Gardens, Pittsburgh, Pennsylvania: http://www.phipps.conservatory.org
Planting Fields Arboretum State Historic Park, Oyster Bay, New York: http://www.plantingfields.org
Scott Arboretum of Swarthmore College, Swarthmore, Pennsylvania: http://www.scottarboretum.org
Botanic Garden of Smith College, Northampton, Massachusetts: http://www.smith.edu/garden/home.html
United States Botanic Garden, Washington, D.C.: http://www.usbg.gov

Indoor poinsettia display at Planting Fields Arboretum State Historic Park

Glossary

Plants that provide exceptional winter interest have a specific role in enhancing the garden. It is important to be familiar with the following landscape terms in order to understand the function, cultural requirements, and ornamental value of trees and shrubs.

Accent: Accent plantings are attractive trees and shrubs that will add interest to the garden. Accent plants can offer interesting bark, foliage, flowers, or fruit and brighten up the landscape. An example would be using a variegated plant to liven up a shady area of the garden.

Background: Shrubs or trees used as backdrops to other plants. They act like a canvas for herbaceous plants and other smaller woody plants. Background plants enhance the overall effect that other companion plants will have in the garden.

Cutback shrub: A shrub that is severely pruned low to the ground annually or every few years in early spring to promote new, vigorous vegetative growth and/or flowers.

Edging plant, or facer: These terms refer to low-growing plants that grow in front of taller plants. These plants are an effective way to give a flower border definition and form.

Foundation planting: Foundation plantings are those shrubs or small trees used near or around the foundation of a house, building, or structure. The purpose of foundation plantings is to soften harsh architectural lines, textures, or colors and to create seasonal interest in a highly visible area.

Groupings: Groupings are strategically placed shrubs or trees in small groups to accomplish a harmonious planting. If room is limited and a large quantity of shrubs are not necessary, a smaller grouping will maintain harmony on a smaller scale. Groupings in odd numbers such as three, five, or seven can provide a less formal look.

Hedges, informal and formal: Woody plants used as hedges must have several important qualities. First, they must be low branched, multistemmed, and dense. Hedges are typically medium to fast growing and form a solid block of growth that can hide or enhance a view, depending on the need. Informal hedges are normally planted in straight or staggered rows, but the plants are allowed to grow in their natural form with little or no pruning. This results in a very graceful, pleasing mound of foliage, stems, flowers, and fruit, depending on the season. Formal hedges are planted in formal arrangement and are sheared regularly to create a very dense, formal appearance. This type of pruning will result in a formal, thick layer of growth.

Mass plantings: The use of one type of shrub or tree in significant quantities will create harmony and maximize the effect these woody plants can have in the landscape. Mass plantings are meant to create a natural rhythm that is pleasing to the eye and is often more attractive than one tree or shrub planted alone. Mass plantings are meant to be seen from a distance and can provide additional function as a barrier or living screen.

Screening: Shrubs and trees used as screening plants function as a physical and visual barrier in the landscape. Their purpose is to hide a specific view, create privacy, or even act as a buffer to wind or noise. Evergreens or densely branched deciduous shrubs should be selected for this purpose.

Specimen planting: A specimen plant typically refers to one individual plant that is attractive and noticeable enough to stand alone in the landscape and is placed where it can be seen clearly. These strategically placed trees and shrubs are considered focal points or main attractions in the garden. In large gardens, several specimens may be clumped together to create a bolder impact.

Other Important Garden Terms

Bract: A modified leaf often associated with a flower. Bracts are typically colorful and are many times confused with flower petals.

Catkin: A spikelike, thin, scaly flower that occurs in the birch and willow families. Male catkins provide ornamental value in the winter.

Compost: Compost is a rich, organic material comprised of humus and other organic material used to improve soil.

Conifer: A plant bearing cones, such as pine, spruce, and fir.

Cultivar: A cultivated variety or garden variety of garden origin. They have very specific ornamental characteristics that are valuable in the cultivated garden.

Deciduous: Deciduous trees and shrubs shed their leaves at the end of the growing season and regain them at the beginning of the next growing season, usually in spring.

Dioecious: Male and female flowers borne on separate plants. Sumac and holly are examples of dioecious plants.

Ericaceous: Relating to or being a member of the heath family, such as heath, rhododendron, pieris, and mountain laurel. Ericaceous plants thrive in well-drained, moist, acidic, organic soil.

Exfoliating bark: Shedding or peeling bark of a tree or shrub. This is considered an attractive feature and adds winter interest. Some plants with exfoliating bark are birch, stewartia, and some maples.

Evergreen: Evergreens are plants that retain their leaves throughout the year and often for more than one year.

Lenticel: Lenticels are small, irregular glands on the bark and stems of plants that allow gas exchange between the plant tissue and the atmosphere. On trees such as birch and cherry, lenticels are very noticeable and are usually arranged horizontally on the branches.

Mycorrhizae: Beneficial soilborne fungi that form a symbiotic relationship with plants. These fungi live in and around roots and help plants absorb needed nutrients and water from the soil.

Mulch: A layer of material, usually organic, applied to the soil surface to suppress weeds, retain soil moisture, moderate soil temperature, and add organic matter to the soil.

Samara: A dry, winged fruit with a seed, such as produced by maples and elms.

Soil pH: A measure of alkalinity or acidity of soils. The pH is measured by a scale from 1–14, with 1 being the most acidic and 14 being the most alkaline. A pH reading of 7 is considered neutral.

Variegated foliage: Leaves striped, edged, or marked with a color different from the primary color of the leaf. Variegation can be creamy white, gold, and other showy colors.

Bibliography

Cedar Site, The. "All About Cedar: What Is a True Cedar?"
    http://www.thecedarsite.com/true-cedar.html (accessed April 5, 2005).

American Rhododendron Society. http://www.rhododendron.org
    (accessed April 5, 2005).

Beaulieu, David. "Christmas Holly Trees: History, Winter Solstice"
    http://landscaping.about.com/cs/winterlandscaping1/a/holly_trees.htm (accessed October 23, 2004).

Bailey Hortorium. *Hortus III.* New York: Macmillan. 1976.

Camellia Forest Nursery. http://www.camforest.com (accessed April 5, 2005).

Cornell Cooperative Extension of Nassau County. Home Horticulture Fact Sheets.
    http://www.ccenassau.org/hort/html/fact_sheets_home_hort.html
    (accessed April 6, 2005).

Dave's Garden. Garden terms. http://davesgarden.com/terms/ (accessed April 5, 2005).

Dirr, Michael A. *Dirr's Hardy Trees and Shrubs.* Portland, Ore.: Timber Press. 1997.

————. *Manual of Woody Landscape Plants.* Fifth edition. Champaign, Ill.:
    Stipes. 1998.

Drzewucki Jr., Vincent. *Gardening in Deer Country.* New York: Brick Tower Press. 1998.

Dudgeon, Doug. "Harry Lauder's Walking-stick"
    http://www.dawesarb.org/main.htm?potm/corylus_avellana_contorta.htm&2.
    (accessed September 15, 2004).

Fisher, Kathleen. "Cold Hardy Camellias." *The American Gardener.* November/
    December 2002. 39–43.

Feucht, J. R. "Evergreen Shrubs for Home Grounds."
    http://www.ext.colostate.edu/pubs/garden/07414.html (accessed October 18, 2004).

Floridata. *"Magnolia grandiflora."* from http://www.floridata.com/ref/m/magno_g.cfm (accessed August 23, 2004).

Gay Gardener Online. Gardening Quotes. http://www.gaygardener.com/quotes.phtml (accessed September 5, 2004).

Imbornoni, Ann-Marie. "Solstice Time." http://www.infoplease.com/spot/wintersolstice1.html (accessed October 4, 2004).

Jaynes, Richard. *Kalmia: Mountain Laurel and Related Species.* Portland, Ore.: Timber Press. 1997.

Kelly, John. *The Hillier Gardener's Guide to Trees and Shrubs.* New York: Readers Digest. 1995.

Knowles, George. "In Worship of Trees. Oak." http://www.controverscial.com/Oak.htm (accessed October 14, 2004).

National Arbor Day Foundation. "Redwood, Dawn." http://www.arborday.org/trees/ treeguide/TreeDetail.cfm?ID=16 (accessed October 30, 2004).

Paghat. "Winter Honeysuckle, aka: Fragrant Honeysuckle, Sweet Breath of Spring, or January Jasmine." http://www.paghat.com/winterhoneysuckle.html (accessed April 6, 2005).

Phillips, Roger. *Trees of North America and Europe: A Photographic Guide to More Than 500 Trees.* New York: Random House. 1993.

Prance, Ghillean Tolmie, and Anne E. Prance. *Bark: The Formation, Characteristics and Uses of bark Around the World.* Portland, Ore.: Timber Press. 1993.

SavATree. "Recuperating from Winter Injury." http://www.savatree.com/pages/timelytips_pages/ timelytips_subsection_pages/timelytips_articles/articles_treehealth/timelytips_recuperating.html (accessed April 5, 2005).

Spirit of Gardening, The. http://www.gardendigest.com/ (accessed September 29, 2004).

Starbuck, Christopher J. "Selecting Landscape Plants: Needled Evergreens." http://muextension.missouri.edu/explore/agguides/hort/g06815.htm (accessed October 11, 2004).

Street, John. *Rhododendrons.* Exeter, U.K.: Justin Knowles Publishing, 1987.

University of Edinburgh. "Taxol, an Anticancer Drug, Is Found in the Pacific Yew." http://www.portfolio.mvm.ed.ac.uk/studentwebs/session2/group13/taxol.html (accessed October 30, 2004).

University of Illinois Extension. "Anti-Desiccants." http://www.solutions.uiuc.edu/
content.cfm?series=4&item=611&Parents=0%7C72 (accessed November 3, 2004).

Vertrees, J. D. *Japanese Maples*. Second edition. Portland, Ore.: Timber Press. 1987.

Virginia Camellia Society. "Very Cold Hardy Camellias." http://members.cox.net/vacs/cold_hardy.htm
(accessed January 29, 2004).

Welch, William C. "Winter Honeysuckle, *Lonicera fragrantissima.*" http://aggie-horticulture.tamu.
edu/southerngarden/lonicera.html (accessed September 2, 2004).

Wildman, Art. *"Hamamelis* spp.—Witch Hazel."
http://www.greenmediaonline.com/aa/1998/0398/0398tm.html (accessed October 14, 2004).

Winter Wisdom. http://ourbigbluemarble.com/themes/tq-winter.htm (accessed October 23, 2004).

WordIQ.com. "Definition of Evergreen." from http://www.wordiq.com/definition/Evergreen
(accessed October 2, 2004).

World of Quotes. Oak quotes. http://www.worldofquotes.com/topic/Oak/1/ (accessed September 17, 2004).

Index of Scientific Plant Names

Index of Common Plant Names

About the Collaborators

Vincent A. Simeone has worked in the horticultural field for over seventeen years. He has horticultural degrees from Farmingdale State University and the University of Georgia. He also has a master's degree from the C.W. Post Campus of Long Island University. Vincent has specialized expertise in woody plant identification, plant culture, landscape use, and selection of superior varieties. Vincent is also an experienced lecturer, teacher, horticultural consultant, and passionate garden writer. He continues to promote innovative trends in gardening such as proper plant selection, four-season gardening, integrated pest management, historic landscape preservation, and low-maintenance gardening.

Vincent teaches a diverse assortment of gardening classes and has assisted in special garden tours to many beautiful gardens in southern England, northern France, southern Germany, Canada, New Zealand, and South Africa. Vincent is also very active in the community on local, regional, and national level with garden clubs, horticultural trade associations, and public garden organizations. Vincent currently works in public horticulture, managing Planting Fields Arboretum State Historic Park in Oyster Bay, New York.

Bruce Richard Curtis has chronicled many of the significant events of the last decades of the twentieth century as a photographer for *Time*, *LIFE*, and *Sports Illustrated*. He has

Vincent A. Simeone and Bruce Richard Curtis

been on the front lines of the Vietnam War, covered the explorations of Jacques Cousteau, captured the glory of the Papal Archives, and chronicled the action on fast-paced sports fields.

His uncanny ability to capture the significant moment led Bruce to explore special effects with MIT physicist and Nobel laureate Dr. Harold Edgerton. His interest in action photography inspired Bruce to use pyrotechnics and laser light to create the "action still life," a combination of the best of special effects and still life photography in one dynamic image. The demand for his images in posters, calendars, books, greeting cards, and CD-ROMs continues to grow. Bruce's studio is located on Long Island, New York.